JACQUES PÉPIN'S KITCHEN

Cooking with Claudine

COMPANION TO THE PUBLIC TELEVISION SERIES

JACQUES PÉPIN'S KITCHEN

Cooking with Claudine

BY JACQUES PÉPIN

DESIGN BY BARBARA MARKS
PHOTOGRAPHS BY PENINA

PRODUCTION OF THE PUBLIC TELEVISION SERIES
JACQUES PÉPIN'S KITCHEN
IS MADE POSSIBLE BY GENEROUS GRANTS FROM
BRAUN INC.   CAMBRIA WINERY & VINEYARD   OXO INTERNATIONAL   RUSSELL RANGE, INC.

KQED
BOOKS
SAN FRANCISCO

CREDITS

Publisher:
   James Connolly
Editorial Director:
   Pamela Byers
Book Designer
and Art Director:
   Barbara Marks
Editor:
   Trent Duffy
Assistants to
Jacques Pépin:
   Norma Galehouse
   Tina Salter
Photographer:
   Penina
Food and Prop Stylist:
   Heidi Gintner
Assistant Stylist:
   Lorraine Battle
Photography Chefs:
   Gary Danko
   Jack Ervin
   Laura Ammons
Cover Portrait:
   Penina
Props provided by:
   Draeger's Market
   Sandra Griswold
   Sue Fisher King
Menu Illustrations by:
   Jacques Pépin
   Claudine Pépin

© 1996 by Jacques Pépin
Illustrations © 1996 by Jacques Pépin

KQED Books & Video, 2601 Mariposa St., San Francisco, CA 94110.

Portions of the material in this book have previously appeared in Jacques Pépin's *New York Times* column, "The Purposeful Cook."

Educational and nonprofit groups wishing to order this book at attractive quantity discounts may contact KQED Books & Video, 2601 Mariposa St., San Francisco, CA 94110.

Library of Congress Cataloguing-in-Publication Data

Pépin, Jacques.
      Jacques Pépin's kitchen: cooking with Claudine / Jacques Pépin; photographs by Penina; design by Barbara Marks.
         p.   cm.
      "Companion to the Public Television series."
      Includes index.
      ISBN: 0-912333-87-1 (pb)
      1. Cookery.   2. Menus.   I. Title.   II. Series: Jacques Pépin's kitchen (Television program)
      TX714.P456   1996   96-42377
      641.5—dc20   CIP

ISBN: 0-912333-87-1 (paperback)
ISBN: 0-912333-84-7 (hardcover)

Manufactured in Hong Kong

10 9 8 7 6 5 4 3 2

Distributed to the trade by Publishers Group West

to daughters and the pleasure of cooking with them -

Contents

Cooking Light

Menus for Special Occasions

Pépin Family Favorites

Recipes by Course

Acknowledgments

Most people do not realize the scope and complexity of producing a television series of twenty-six shows and a companion book. It is not possible to name everyone involved in these projects, but many were absolutely essential to the result and the realization of *Cooking with Claudine.*

I first and foremost want to thank my partner and cohost, my daughter, *Claudine;* I'm proud to say that she turned out to be better than I am on television and was a bridge between me and the audience in that she could explain to them in better English than mine what I was doing. These few weeks we spent together were truly very fine.

I am grateful, too, to *Peter Stein,* the executive producer of the series (alas, I didn't have time to see as much of him as I did when we worked together on previous series); *Peggy Lee Scott,* my producer, who organized all the complicated details and brought everyone together; *Tina Salter,* who was indispensable to me as the liaison between the back kitchen and the set, and whose grace and gentleness kept us all sane; codirectors *Linda Giannecchini,* who, under stressful conditions, took on the challenge and succeeded brilliantly, and *Brian Murphy,* who gave a style to our show but, unfortunately, wasn't around to see it completed; *Leslee Newcomb,* the makeup artist who helped me look good on camera, always with a gentle word and a smile; *Katherine Zilavy,* associate producer, who worked so hard behind the scenes; and *Mari Gill,* assistant to the producer, whose attention to detail was invaluable and who happily chauffeured us around. I also want to thank *Heidi Gintner,* our food and prop stylist, who, after working with me on several series, still manages to come up with new and beautiful arrangements, and her assistant, *Lorraine Battle,* who was always ready to help and lend her expertise.

I am extremely indebted to the back kitchen staff, whose help was essential to the success of the show. First, I thank my friend, the chef and kitchen manager, *Gary Danko,* who worked very closely with Tina and me to synchronize the show, and all of his able helpers: *Laura Ammons, Joseph Strebler, Mike Pleiss, Eiji Kawashima, Bernice Chunk Fong, Jack Ervin, Kasey Kobayashi,* and *Helen Soehalim,* as well as their student assistants, *Carol Heuser* and *Charlie Vollmar.*

The series led us, of course, to the production of this book, and, for their help on this project I want to thank: *Norma Galehouse,* my longtime assistant, for her dedication and proficiency at the difficult job of putting all the material together; my wife, *Gloria,* for tasting the food and advising me; *James Connolly,* publisher, and *Pamela Byers,* editorial director, KQED Books & Video, for their professionalism and search for quality on this book project; *Barbara Marks,* my friend and neighbor, for her beautiful design and art direction of the book; *Penina,* my photographer, whose great eye gave us not only the wonderful pictures of Claudine and me on the cover and throughout the book, but made all the food look absolutely terrific; *Trent Duffy,* our capable editor, for his impeccable attention to detail; and the many other people, known and unknown to me behind the scenes, whose involvement made it all possible.

—JACQUES PÉPIN

A Conversation with Jacques and Claudine

BY JANET FLETCHER

Rejoice, Jacques Pépin fans. The popular French chef is back, this time with an irreverent redheaded *sous*-chef: his daughter, Claudine.

In *Jacques Pépin's Kitchen: Cooking with Claudine,* the companion cookbook for her father's new PBS series, the twenty-eight-year-old Claudine steps into the kitchen for twenty-six cooking lessons designed to enable you and her to eat well and wisely.

By her own admission, Claudine gets by in the kitchen, but with less than professional skills. And she can't quite figure why people expect her to be a fine cook. "If my father were a surgeon, would I necessarily know how to operate?" she asks.

But as the daughter, granddaughter, cousin, and niece of French chefs, she has learned a lot by osmosis—not recipes per se, but a certain sense of good taste and an appreciation for food that's well made.

Now, admits Claudine, it's time to master a few more cooking skills. It would be nice not to repeat the mistake she made a few years ago when her father came to her Boston apartment for dinner. "It was my dad, so I was just going to roast a chicken," recounts Claudine. "I wasn't going to pains. But he was late and I started cooking early—a bad combination. We're sitting there and he's eating his chicken, and I'm thinking, this is terrible. It's overcooked and dry. I looked at him and said, 'What do you think?' He replied, 'As a father . . . or as a chef?' "

Recognizing that many young people like Claudine have minimal funds, limited time, and a contemporary concern for health, Jacques wanted to develop teaching menus that would speak to them. The menus he devised for *Cooking with Claudine* have young adults in mind, but these lessons will make any reader more adept in the kitchen.

In the following pages, you will learn to make a single leg of lamb yield four different dishes; to create an enticing lean meal of steamed scallops and corned beef *pot-au-feu;* and to cook as well for one as for a dozen. Following Jacques' clear explanations, you can light up a tailgate party with Peking-style chicken and corn spoonbread, master a nearly vegetarian menu of Swiss chard–stuffed onions and bulgur and mint salad, or further a romance with a goat cheese soufflé and veal *blanquette.*

Cooking with Claudine will also appeal if you share Claudine's need for economy (she's still in graduate school) or Jacques' deep-seated distaste for waste. "I go crazy throwing things out," admits the chef, whose resourceful French mother never discarded so much as a sprig of parsley. He doesn't either; instead, he shares with readers and viewers the idea of *cuisine d'opportunité,* a way of cooking that makes the most of what you have.

In one lesson, he transforms the odds and ends in Claudine's refrigerator into a wholesome meal for her visiting friends: vegetable soup with grits, a French country omelet, and a colorful carrot, zucchini, and radish salad. "It looks like I planned it," says an impressed Claudine, surveying her father's improvisations with what had seemed like slim pickings. And for dessert? Well, she does have some very old bananas. "If that's all you have, that's all we use," says Jacques, who swiftly turns the sad-looking fruit into sugar-dusted fritters.

"If you can use leftovers well, you have an understanding of food that's more important than being able to decorate a plate," argues Jacques. "Using leftovers may seem humble or ordinary, but it shows a cook's imagination. It's part of my upbringing, and it's the approach of any good cook."

In this new book and television series, Jacques also passes on to his daughter recipes from Pépin family tradition: the bread and butter pudding that Jacques' wife, Gloria, requests for her birthday; grandmother Jeannette's famous apple tart; a black bean soup that reflects Gloria's Caribbean heritage; and the clam fritters and broiled stuffed lobster that remind Claudine of childhood summers at the New England shore.

These dishes shared *en famille* create vivid taste memories that tie us together, says Jacques. "There's that famous scene in Proust's *Remembrance of Things Past,*" recalls the chef, who has a master's degree in French literature. "The narrator is tasting a madeleine and some tea, and out of this tea comes the memory of his youth—his grandmother, and his garden, and the priest next door. The whole town comes out of this cup of tea."

That's the affective memory at work, as opposed to the intellect, says Jacques. "It assails you when you don't expect it, and it's brought about by the senses—by a smell, a taste, a view. It's powerful and immediate, and it will follow you the rest of your life."

For Claudine, who grew up in the kitchen, many dishes provoke warm family memories. A taste of bread and onion soup can transport her to her grandmother's comfortable kitchen table in France, where she spent summers and Christmas holidays. "I can make the soup. My father can make it. Anybody can make it," says Claudine. "But it's never as good as when my grandmother makes it."

In France, surrounded by her father's food-loving aunts, uncles, and cousins, Claudine learned how important food traditions can be in connecting a family. And as a child at home in Connecticut, washing the vegetables for her father or clipping herbs for him from the garden, she slowly absorbed his preference for simple cooking that pleases and nurtures without straining to impress.

"There are very few things in the kitchen that we disagree on," says Claudine, "except that I say if I eat standing up, there are no calories. . . . Oh, and he says I don't serve the food with enough love. I take the plate; I put the food on it. He looks at me, saying, 'Claudine, you should show more love for the food.' I guess my presentation could get better."

No doubt some of Jacques' artful eye has rubbed off on his daughter during these twenty-six cooking lessons. The six weeks spent rehearsing and taping the shows in San Francisco provided the two of them with the opportunity to spend the kind of time together that few fathers and adult daughters have. "I wouldn't have asked her to do the project if I didn't think she was capable," says Jacques, "but she is very good and natural at television." A hit with viewers when she appeared previously on shows with her dad, Claudine agreed to take a break from Boston University, where she's pursuing a master's in international relations, to spend part of her summer in a television studio.

She agrees that she's comfortable in front of the camera but admits to some hair-raising moments. Chief among them was the day the crew tried to film her getting on and off a train for use as an opening scene for the series. With camera crew gathered at the San Francisco train station and a train pulling in, producer Peggy Scott called for a trial run. "What I was supposed to do is get on the train and get off the train," recalls Claudine. "To me, that means two doors, so it will look realistic. So I get on the train and run down the aisle, but as soon as I get to the other door—*boom*. They close it. I'm off to Redwood City. I have no identification, I have no money, and I have a lot of makeup on. I beg the conductor, 'Please! Stop the train!' When I get off, Peggy is white and my father is laughing hysterically. And I say, 'Well, I guess that woke everybody up.'"

On the set, Claudine sees her role as that of the voice of the people, asking the questions that most home cooks have: "Can I freeze it? Can I make it ahead? Is it going to be expensive? How long is this going to take?"

As Jacques' willing but not-that-able assistant, she inevitably makes mistakes that her father turns into learning experiences. When she peels a carrot the way most home cooks do, Jacques shows her a faster professional method. When she shatters a raw egg on the cutting board, he doesn't miss a beat, swiftly scooting it into the proper bowl with his hand. "Awesome," says Claudine.

"That's how you teach," says Jacques. It's one thing to show students the right way to do a kitchen task. But it's equally helpful if they can see a mistake being corrected. "They see the type of recovery that happens when you know how to cook," says the chef. In that sense, *Cooking with Claudine* may be the most informative work yet from this renowned teacher.

His fans will recognize in this engaging recipe collection the Jacques Pépin stamp: a complete lack of fuss and pretension. His down-to-earth attitude about cooking contradicts our image of the demanding French chef, but Claudine insists he really does take pleasure in simple things. "He taught me never to be a snob about food," says his daughter. "Everything has merit—every culture's food, every type of food. A meal doesn't have to be three-star caliber to be enjoyable. If it's simple, fresh, and good, you can find pleasure in it—probably more pleasure, in fact, because your attention is focused more on the people you're eating with and less on the food. Unfortunately, I think a lot of people go from peanut butter to haute cuisine and miss what's in the middle."

You'll find plenty of "in the middle" dishes in the following pages—inviting, everyday recipes like shoulder steak with herbs, cold corn soup, spicy ginger and lemon chicken, or ziti with sausage and vegetables. But Jacques also proposes menus for more important occasions when you might want to take what Claudine would call more "pains." Who wouldn't appreciate a birthday dinner of ricotta dumplings with red pepper sauce, followed by Russian-style Cornish hens? And if you are angling for a promotion or a raise, Jacques has a menu that might do the trick. Invite your boss for polenta and vegetable *gâteau,* escalopes of veal in mushroom and Cognac sauce, carrot crêpes, and strawberry *clafoutis.*

But even his more ambitious menus are within the reach of novice cooks, because Jacques is an irrepressible teacher. On the screen and on the page, he makes challenging steps easy, sharing shortcuts and chef's tricks because he's so eager to get people into the kitchen. "You miss a lot by not knowing how to cook," insists Jacques, who believes the kitchen should be the heart of the home. "I know families that hardly say two words to one another, but they don't realize it. They pass each other while they grab a sandwich, but they never have a conversation. The table is the place where you talk about school and about all the other family things. Sometimes it's not that pleasant, but it is very necessary."

Words of wisdom from a kitchen philosopher with many thought-provoking notions on food. So pull up a chair in *Jacques Pépin's Kitchen: Cooking with Claudine* and, along with Claudine, enjoy the benefits of her father's enthusiastic teaching. Then head into your own kitchen to create the taste memories that will enrich your own life, and those of your family.

On Menus and Wines

When organizing my books, I'm somewhat reluctant to suggest menus and specific wines to accompany these menus because, more often than not, my suggestions are interpreted as "laws" that must be obeyed. I think there is something presumptuous about deciding for others what dish goes well with other dishes in the making of a menu and, on top of that, then telling them what wine they should serve with this menu. However, the alternative—providing no suggestions at all—is vacuous and often leaves the reader perplexed and empty-handed.

Therefore, this book is divided into menus with wine suggestions. Use this information for guidance only, changing the recipe groupings and substituting other wines at will to suit your lifestyle or mood. On a daily basis, I decide on a menu while in the market looking at produce. I take into account season, availability, price, and special sales, as well as my humor and the disposition of my eating partners.

Feel free to reorganize the dishes in my menus. Add or eliminate dishes to fit your own tastes or habits. At my house, for example, we always enjoy salad and bread with our meals, but rarely have desserts other than fresh fruits. Wine is conventionally served with all our meals.

The range of wines available, in terms of quality and price, is immense. In the menu "A Lesson in Economy," I mention a Spanish and a French wine, both of very good quality and particularly low in price. At the other end of the scale, the wines suggested in "Birthday Party for Mom" are for a special meal, when you want to splurge. Once in a while, as in the "Family Celebration" menu, I suggest a dessert wine.

Most of all, one should never lose the focus of what food is about. In addition to its physiological function, food is togetherness, identity, and culture. It is the glue that holds the family together.

The Busy Single

Easy Short-Cut Supper

Greens and Sardine Salad

Shoulder Steak with Herbs

Roasted Potatoes and Onions

Soda Bread

Blueberries "au Citron"

Jacques 96

It is useful to know how to prepare quick, simple meals for those days when you get home late from work but still want to have a nice dinner.

This menu is fast, easy, and inexpensive to make. Be sure to turn on the oven first, and start with the bread and the potato and onion dish, both of which need time to cook.

The meal begins with green salad containing diced plum tomatoes and sardines. Cut into small pieces and tossed with the salad greens at the last moment to add a special zest, the sardines make the salad a bit more complete and sophisticated.

My main course features economical beef shoulder steaks, which are sautéed in olive oil and finished with garlic, herbs, and a little butter. When I prepare this dish in the summer, I use an assortment of fresh herbs~tarragon, chives, and parsley~plucked straight from my garden as a garnish.

The steaks are served with oven-roasted potatoes and onions in a simple recipe that uses much less oil than if the ingredients were fried or sautéed in a skillet: Only $1^{1}/_{2}$ tablespoons of oil are required to roast 4 potatoes and 4 onions. The oil is spread out on a large, heavy aluminum cookie sheet or jelly roll pan, and the potatoes and onions, both halved, are arranged cut side down on the greased pan.

CLAUDINE:
~

"Steak and potatoes are just basic, good food. It's everything you want. It's American food."

Most breads take hours to make. The exception is a classic soda bread, which can be ready for the oven in a matter of minutes. Any leftover bread is good toasted.

Blueberries, simply flavored with lemon juice and maple syrup, are the perfect finish for this quickly prepared meal.

WINE

RED

Rosemount Estate, Shiraz

Special Tip

If you have access to a barbecue grill, the steaks are great grilled. Use the same ingredient amounts as called for in the recipe, brush the steaks with the olive oil, season them with the salt and pepper, and grill them to your liking. Combine the butter and herbs in a small bowl and, just before the steaks are served, spoon the flavored butter mixture on top of them to melt and flavor the steaks.

Greens and Sardine Salad

Use a variety of salad greens in this dish, and take care to wash them properly: After gently agitating the greens in a sink full of cold water, lift them from the water, drain them thoroughly, and dry—preferably in a salad spinner. Thorough drying is necessary because water will dilute the dressing and render the salad tasteless. I love canned sardines, preferring the plump ones from Portugal or the southwest of France.

TOTAL TIME
20 minutes

YIELD
4 servings

NUTRITIONAL ANALYSIS PER SERVING

Calories 193
Protein 6.7 gm.
Carbohydrates 7.4 gm.
Fat 15.6 gm.
Saturated fat 2.5 gm.
Cholesterol 9.2 mg.
Sodium 266.6 mg.

1 **(4-ounce) can sardines in olive oil**

½ **cup chopped onion**

3 **plum tomatoes, cut into 1-inch dice (1½ cups)**

2½ **tablespoons virgin olive oil**

1½ **tablespoons red wine vinegar**

¼ **teaspoon salt**

¼ **teaspoon freshly ground black pepper**

5 **cups salad greens (Boston lettuce, escarole, and other varieties), trimmed, rinsed, and thoroughly dried**

1 Reserving the juices and oil in the can, cut the sardines into 1-inch pieces. Place the pieces in a large salad bowl, and add the reserved juices and oil. Add all the remaining ingredients except the greens to the bowl, and mix them together gently.

2 At serving time, add the greens to the bowl, toss to coat them with the dressing, and divide among four plates for serving. (Alternatively, arrange the greens on individual plates or on a large platter, and spoon the sardine mixture on top.)

Shoulder Steak with Herbs

These small beef steaks, each weighing 5 to 6 ounces, are from the shoulder blade. Very lean, they have a large sinewy nerve running through the center that becomes deliciously gelatinous and chewy when cooked. Cooked quickly—either sautéed as here, or grilled—they are juicy and flavorful. Braised whole, this same piece of meat makes a delicious pot roast, and it is also great cut into pieces and cooked in a stew.

4   beef shoulder blade steaks (chicken steaks), 5 to 6 ounces each

1½ teaspoons virgin olive oil

¼   teaspoon salt

¼   teaspoon freshly ground black pepper

2   tablespoons chopped shallots

⅓   cup water

1   tablespoon unsalted butter

¼   cup fresh herbs (tarragon, chives, parsley, etc.), finely chopped

1   Heat a large, sturdy skillet (cast iron or heavy-duty aluminum, not nonstick). Brush the steaks on both sides with the oil, sprinkle them with the salt and pepper, and place them in the hot skillet. Cook for 2 to 3 minutes over medium to high heat on each side for 1-inch steaks (medium-rare).

2   Remove the steaks from the skillet, and place them on a platter. Add the shallots to the drippings in the skillet, and sauté them for 20 seconds. Add the water to the skillet, mix it in well, and cook, stirring, until all the encrusted juices in the skillet have melted.

3   Add the butter and the herbs to the mixture in the skillet, and cook for a few seconds, just until the butter melts.

4   Spoon the butter/herb mixture over the steaks, and serve immediately.

   Note: The steaks can be kept for 10 to 15 minutes in a 180-degree oven before serving. If doing this, however, finish step 2, then wait until plating the steaks before adding the butter and herbs to the drippings in the skillet.

TOTAL TIME
10 minutes

YIELD
4 servings

NUTRITIONAL ANALYSIS PER SERVING

Calories 277.5
Protein 30.3 gm.
Carbohydrates 1.1 gm.
Fat 16.1 gm.
Saturated fat 6.3 gm.
Cholesterol 109.1 mg.
Sodium 257.0 mg.

Roasted Potatoes and Onions

To save on cleaning time, line the jelly roll pan with aluminum foil. Baked cut side down in a minimum of oil (much of the oil remains in the pan afterward), the potatoes emerge brown and moist, and have far fewer calories than a conventional fried potato or baked potato topped with sour cream.

TOTAL TIME
50 minutes

YIELD
4 servings

NUTRITIONAL ANALYSIS PER SERVING

Calories 269.8
Protein 7.3 gm.
Carbohydrates 50.8 gm.
Fat 5.5 gm.
Saturated fat 0.9 gm.
Cholesterol 0 mg.
Sodium 166.0 mg.

4 **baking or all-purpose potatoes (about 8 ounces each), left unpeeled, but washed and any dark or damaged spots removed**

4 **medium onions (about 5 ounces each), left unpeeled (Vidalia or Maui onions are a good choice)**

1½ **tablespoons peanut or safflower oil**

¼ **teaspoon salt**

1 Preheat the oven to 400 degrees.

2 Split the potatoes in half lengthwise, and cut the onions in half crosswise.

3 Pour the oil on an aluminum jelly roll pan. Sprinkle the salt over the potatoes and onions, and place them cut side down in one layer on the oiled pan.

4 Place the pan on the bottom rack of the 400-degree oven (or, if you want the underside of your vegetables very crusty, on the oven floor). Bake for 40 minutes, until the potatoes and onions are tender when pierced with a fork, lightly browned on top, and dark brown on the underside.

5 Set the potatoes and onions aside to rest for 10 minutes, lift with a spatula, and serve.

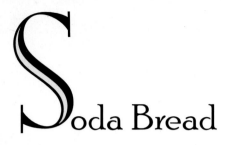

Soda Bread

When pressed for time, soda bread is the perfect solution. This British classic requires only a few minutes of work to put together. In fact, if you turn on your oven before starting to combine the ingredients, the bread will be ready to bake by the time the oven reaches temperature. No proofing is necessary—the bread should be baked immediately after it is assembled for the baking powder to work effectively.

Soda bread is conventionally made with buttermilk and baking soda, but I achieve the same result here with regular milk and baking powder. If you want to make the classic version, use the same amounts of buttermilk and baking soda.

Covering the dough with an inverted stainless steel bowl during the first 30 minutes of baking creates a moist environment in which it can rise. Then, after the bowl is removed, the crust of the bread hardens and browns.

TOTAL TIME
1 hour 15 minutes

YIELD
6 to 8 servings

NUTRITIONAL ANALYSIS PER SERVING

Calories 230.3
Protein 7.3 gm.
Carbohydrates 43.6 gm.
Fat 2.6 gm.
Saturated fat 1.2 gm.
Cholesterol 7.3 mg.
Sodium 601.8 mg.

3 **cups all-purpose flour**
1½ **teaspoons salt**
1½ **teaspoons baking powder**
1½ **cups milk**
½ **teaspoon canola oil**

1 Preheat the oven to 425 degrees.

2 Reserve 1 teaspoon of the flour, and combine the remaining flour with the salt and baking powder in a large mixing bowl. Add the milk, and mix gently and quickly with a wooden spatula until the mixture forms into a solid mass.

3 Oil an aluminum nonstick baking sheet with the canola oil, and place the dough on the sheet. Using a piece of plastic wrap, press and mold the dough to create a round loaf about 7 inches in diameter and 1 inch thick. Sprinkle the reserved teaspoon of flour on top of the loaf, and, using a serrated knife, make two

intersecting ¼-inch-deep cuts across the top surface of the loaf to create a cross.

4 Place a stainless steel bowl upside down over the bread, and place it in the 425-degree oven for 30 minutes. Uncover, and cook at the same temperature for another 30 minutes.

5 Using a hamburger spatula, remove the bread from the baking sheet, and set it aside to cool on a rack for at least 30 minutes before slicing and serving.

Blueberries *au Citron*

We finish with blueberries flavored simply with lemon juice and maple syrup. Make this dessert only when fresh blueberries are readily available. I find the tiny wild berries more flavorful than the large cultivated ones, so use them whenever possible.

TOTAL TIME
5 minutes, plus
chilling time

YIELD
4 servings

**NUTRITIONAL
ANALYSIS
PER SERVING**

Calories 94.8
Protein 0.5 gm.
Carbohydrates 24.3 gm.
Fat 0.3 gm.
Saturated fat 0 gm.
Cholesterol 0 mg.
Sodium 6.3 mg.

1 **lemon**
¼ **cup maple syrup**
1 **pint (12 ounces) blueberries,
preferably small wild ones**

1 Using a vegetable peeler, remove 4 peels from the lemon, and set them aside. Cut the lemon in half, and press it to obtain the juice (about 2 tablespoons).

2 Mix the lemon juice and maple syrup in a bowl large enough to hold the blueberries.

3 Rinse the blueberries well in cool water, removing and discarding any damaged berries or foreign matter. Drain the berries well, and add them to the syrup mixture along with the lemon peel. Mix well, and refrigerate for at least 1 hour before serving.

Pennywise Potluck

Cooked Turkey Carcass Soup

Cumin Lamb breast and Potatoes

Mushrooms "en Papillote"

Cucumber Summer Salad

Fresh Fruit

Jacques 96

A good cook knows that a delicious meal can be prepared with very little money if one has a good sense of taste and a basic knowledge of cooking. Be sure to use your market to good advantage; walk up and down the aisles looking for specials and reduced items before finalizing your menu.

My family loves roast turkey, not only at Thanksgiving, but as a main dish for company year-round. Each time we prepare it, my wife makes turkey carcass soup afterward with a stock she creates from the cooked turkey bones. Sometimes she adds pasta and vegetables to the stock, as in the recipe I present; other times, she thickens the stock with a light roux and stirs in some spinach or another green.

The main course is cumin lamb breast and potatoes. Based on your taste preferences and your tolerance for highly seasoned foods, use more or less chili powder than is called for in the recipe. I also include apples (which I usually have on hand), chopping them and adding them, skin and all, to the lamb. In addition to serving as a binding agent in the sauce, they impart a sweet taste that contrasts appealingly with the hot flavor of the dish. For a nice finish, I add lemon zest and parsley at the end.

Mushrooms are featured in the interesting side dish I serve with the lamb. Enclosed in aluminum foil, whole mushrooms and slices of garlic bake in the oven while the lamb breast cooks on top of the stove. A refreshing cucumber salad follows. The meal is finished simply with whatever fresh fruit is in season. There's no recipe for this dessert – just shop wisely and improvise.

WINE

RED

Viña Calina, Merlot

CLAUDINE:

~

"My father's approach to economy in the kitchen is that if it's not the plastic wrap that it came in, you have *to eat it. . . . You have to use it. He'll use things that I would never consider using."*

Cooked Turkey Carcass Soup

This soup can be made with uncooked turkey bones, which are available at most markets, but my family prefers it made with the bones from a roast turkey. Any leftover, solidified juices or vegetable garnishes from the roast turkey—a clove of garlic, perhaps, or pieces of onion—are also added to the stock as flavor enhancers.

TOTAL TIME

3 hours

YIELD

4 to 6 servings

NUTRITIONAL ANALYSIS PER SERVING

Calories 151.3
Protein 8.3 gm.
Carbohydrates 24.2 gm.
Fat 2.9 gm.
Saturated fat 1.3 gm.
Cholesterol 6.0 mg.
Sodium 209.4 mg.

About 2 pounds turkey carcass bones from a cooked turkey, plus any leftover juices and/or cooked garnishes (such as pieces of carrot, onion, or garlic)

4 quarts water

2 carrots (about 6 ounces), peeled and cut into ½-inch pieces (1 cup)

1 medium leek (about 5 ounces), cleaned and cut into 1-inch pieces (greens included) (2 cups)

1 cup diced (½-inch) celery

3 cups coarsely chopped outer lettuce leaves or leftover salad greens

½ cup (about 3 ounces) pastina (any tiny pasta in alphabet, star, or square shapes)

1 Remove all the skin from the turkey carcass. Place all the turkey bones, juice, and cooked garnishes in a large stainless steel stockpot with the water. Bring the water to a strong boil, then skim off and discard as much of the fat and scum from the surface as possible.

2 Reduce the heat, and boil the mixture gently, uncovered, for 2 hours. Strain. This will yield 2 quarts of stock. (Note: If your yield is greater, boil the stock until it is reduced to 2 quarts; if your yield is less, add water to bring up to 2 quarts.) Remove and discard all visible fat from the surface of the stock. Pick the meat from the bones, and add it to the stock.

3 Rinse the stockpot, and place the stock back in the pot with all the remaining ingredients except the pastina. Bring the stock to a boil, reduce the heat to low, cover, and boil gently for 20 minutes. Add the pastina, and continue to boil gently, covered, for another 10 minutes. Serve immediately, or cool completely, and refrigerate or freeze for later use.

Cumin Lamb Breast and Potatoes

Lamb breast—a very flavorful cut—is usually priced quite inexpensively at the market. The breast contains layers of fat, some of which I remove from the top, although I leave the pink-colored fell or pelt. I then cut the breast into riblets, and—possibly the most important technique of this recipe—brown these pieces of meat for a long time in a Dutch oven on top of the stove. This dry cooking extracts most of the remaining fat from the breast, which is crucial because the fat not only has a strong flavor but is highly caloric. The last time I prepared this dish, a full cup of fat was rendered and discarded before I proceeded with the recipe.

TOTAL TIME

1½ **hours**

YIELD

4 **servings**

**NUTRITIONAL
ANALYSIS
PER SERVING**

Calories 649.9
Protein 31.3 gm.
Carbohydrates 42.9 gm.
Fat 39.2 gm.
Saturated fat 16.3 gm.
Cholesterol 123.7 mg.
Sodium 973.1 mg.

2 **lamb breasts (about 2 pounds total)**

2 **medium onions (8 ounces), peeled and chopped (about 2 cups)**

1½ **tablespoons cumin powder**

1 **teaspoon chili powder**

1 **tablespoon tomato paste**

1 **large apple (about 8 ounces), left unpeeled, but cored and coarsely chopped (2½ cups)**

1½ **teaspoons salt**

2 **cups water**

12 **small new potatoes (about 1½ pounds), peeled**

1 **teaspoon grated lemon rind**

1 **tablespoon chopped fresh parsley**

1 Remove most of the visible fat from the top of the lamb breasts (leaving the pinkish fell or skin pelt on top). Cut each breast between the ribs, so that you end up with 8 pieces.

2 Place the ribs in one layer in a large Dutch oven or similar pot, and cook them, covered, over medium heat for about 20 minutes, turning the pieces occasionally, until they are well browned, crisp, and most of the fat has melted from them.

3 Transfer the ribs to a plate, and discard the rendered fat. Place the lamb pieces back in the pot with the onions, and sauté for 1 minute. Add the cumin powder, chili powder, tomato paste, apple, and salt. Mix well, and add the

...il reduce the
...il gently
...
Add the potatoes to the p...
...ook for another 30 minutes.
...e lemon rind
and parsley togeth... in a small
bowl.

6 When the potatoes are tender,
sprinkle the lemon-parsley
mixture over the dish, stir it in,
and serve immediately.

Note: This dish can be cooled
and refrigerated, then reheated at
serving time. However, if you do
so, do not add the lemon-parsley
mixture until just before serving.

Cucumber Summer Salad

This salad of onion, cucumber, dill, and mint makes a refreshing addition to most any
summer menu.

2 cucumbers (about 1¾ pounds),
peeled, seeded, and sliced thin
(about 4 cups)

1 large onion (8 ounces), peeled
and sliced thin (about 2 cups)

⅓ cup shredded fresh dill

⅓ cup shredded fresh mint

1 teaspoon salt

3 tablespoons cider vinegar

1 tablespoon canola oil

2 teaspoons sugar

½ teaspoon Tabasco hot pepper
sauce

1 Combine all the ingredients in a
large bowl. Mix well, and
refrigerate for at least 30 minutes
but as long as 8 hours. (The salad
is best if left for a minimum of
2 to 3 hours.)

2 Serve cool with crunchy bread.

TOTAL TIME
20 minutes, plus
marinating time

YIELD
4 servings

**NUTRITIONAL
ANALYSIS
PER SERVING**
Calories 85.9
Protein 1.8 gm.
Carbohydrates 13.2 gm.
Fat 3.7 gm.
Saturated fat 0.3 gm.
Cholesterol 0 mg.
Sodium 568.1 mg.

Mushrooms *en Papillote*

This recipe couldn't be simpler or tastier. When food is prepared *en papillote,* the French term for "in paper," it generally is baked inside a wrapping of parchment paper. I get the same effect with aluminum foil here; the mushrooms cook and steam inside a foil package, retaining all their flavor and moisture.

TOTAL TIME

1 hour

YIELD

6 servings

NUTRITIONAL ANALYSIS PER SERVING

Calories 61.3
Protein 1.8 gm.
Carbohydrates 4.8 gm.
Fat 4.5 gm.
Saturated fat 1.5 gm.
Cholesterol 5.2 mg.
Sodium 186.4 mg.

1 **pound medium-size mushrooms**

½ **teaspoon salt**

½ **teaspoon freshly ground black pepper**

6 **cloves garlic, peeled and thinly sliced (2 tablespoons)**

1 **tablespoon unsalted butter**

1 **tablespoon virgin olive oil**

1 **tablespoon chopped fresh parsley**

1 Preheat the oven to 400 degrees. Arrange a 16- to 18-inch square of aluminum foil on a flat work surface.

2 Wash the mushrooms, drain them well, and pile them in the center of the foil. Sprinkle them with the salt, pepper, and garlic. Dot with the butter, and then sprinkle with the oil. Gather up the edges of the foil, and fold them together securely to encase the mushrooms in a square package.

3 Place the foil package seam side up on a cookie sheet, and bake in the 400-degree oven for 45 minutes.

4 Unwrap the mushroom package, and serve the mushrooms in their own juices with a sprinkling of parsley on top.

"Cuisine d'opportunité"

Collard Greens and Yellow grits Soup

"Omelette de Campagne"

Carrot, Zucchini, and radish Salad

Banana fritters

Jacques 96

This menu demonstrates how much can be done with ordinary foods that you probably have in your refrigerator. The good cook welcomes the challenge of creating inspirational dishes from simple foods combined in interesting ways.

Hearty soups are very often featured at our table, especially during the cold weather months. I use collard greens in the robust soup that begins this menu, but curly or flat-leaf kale, leftover salad greens, spinach, or the like can be substituted.

When I was a child, we ate eggs more often than we do now. Primarily for economic reasons, they appeared as the main course in our home several times a week in lieu of meat or fish. Concerns over cholesterol have made them a less frequent visitor, but they are rich in protein (and thus still one of the most nutritious  foods on the market) and their reasonable price makes them a good choice occasionally for a main dish.

Here, with the addition of onions, potatoes, and tomatoes, eggs are transformed into a Spanish-style omelet. I recommend buying eggs

...the chickens are fed organically; the cost may be ...tion... ...ots, ze...m, a... ...nd; invar...bly some of this produce is in a stage of decline or ...cay. In thi... menu, the vegetables are trimmed and transformed into a tasty salad.

Banana fritters complete our menu. I prefer well-ripened bananas and look for them with their skins already speckled with black dots at my market. Be sure to prepare the batter with ice water, and, if making it ahead, refrigerate it until you are ready to proceed with the recipe.

WINE

RED

Château de La Chaize,
Brouilly

Special Tip

Leftover soup—like the greens and ...nts soup in this ...u—usually thickens as it cools. For a different presentation the following day, change the texture and ...... of the soup by emulsifying it into a puree in a food processor. Thinned with a little chicken stock, reheated, and served with additional croutons, it is equally as flavorful as it was the first time around, but has a fresh new look and taste.

Collard Greens and Yellow Grits Soup

I thicken this soup with yellow grits, but you can use couscous or another type of grain. If you make the soup ahead and find that it is too thick when reheated, add water to bring it to the desired consistency.

1 tablespoon virgin olive oil

12 ounces collard greens, leaves cut into 1-inch pieces, stems into ½-inch pieces (7 cups, lightly packed), washed and drained

2 carrots (5 ounces), peeled and cut into ½-inch pieces (1 cup)

7 cups chicken stock (or light beef stock), preferably unsalted

1 teaspoon salt (or less, if using salted stock)

⅓ cup yellow grits

1 Heat the oil in a pot. When it is hot, add the drained collard greens, and sauté them over high heat for 4 to 5 minutes, stirring occasionally, until they are wilted.

2 Add the carrots and stock to the pot. Bring to a boil, reduce the heat to low, cover, and boil gently for 15 minutes. Add the salt and yellow grits, cover, and continue to boil the mixture gently for 10 minutes longer. Serve immediately, or cool, cover, refrigerate, and reheat at serving time.

TOTAL TIME
About 45 minutes

YIELD
About 6 to 7 cups

NUTRITIONAL ANALYSIS PER SERVING
Calories 113.3
Protein 5.3 gm.
Carbohydrates 14.7 gm.
Fat 4.2 gm.
Saturated fat 1.2 gm.
Cholesterol 4.4 mg.
Sodium 508.1 mg.

Carrot, Zucchini, and Radish Salad

This salad features carrots, zucchini, and radishes, vegetables that are available year-round. To add variety, the carrots are shredded, the zucchini cut into julienne strips, and the radishes sliced. These vegetables are then mixed with a simple dressing and set aside for a while to soften before they are served.

TOTAL TIME
15 minutes, plus 1
hour marinating time

YIELD
4 servings

NUTRITIONAL ANALYSIS PER SERVING

Calories 137.1
Protein 1.7 gm.
Carbohydrates 9.2 gm.
Fat 11.3 gm.
Saturated fat 1.7 gm.
Cholesterol 8.1 mg.
Sodium 379.9 mg.

DRESSING

¼ cup mayonnaise

1½ tablespoons cider vinegar

½ teaspoon salt

½ teaspoon freshly ground black pepper

3 medium carrots (about 8 ounces), peeled and shredded (about 2¼ cups)

1 zucchini (10 ounces), trimmed, washed, cut lengthwise into ¼-inch-thick slices, then stacked and cut into ¼-inch julienne strips (about 2 cups)

12 radishes (about 5 ounces), cleaned and finely sliced (1 cup)

1 Combine the dressing ingredients in a bowl large enough to hold the salad.

2 Add the prepared vegetables to the dressing, and toss to combine. Let stand for at least 1 hour to slightly soften the vegetables before serving.

Omelette de Campagne

This omelet contains 1½ eggs per person. Essentially, the eggs serve as a binder for thinly sliced raw potatoes and onions, which are first sautéed, then covered with thin slices of tomato. When the eggs are poured into the skillet, they make the vegetables cohere, forming a kind of dish that the Spanish call *tortilla*. Even though we usually serve the omelet hot—often with a salad—at my house, it is also delicious served cool in the Spanish style.

1½ **tablespoons canola oil**

1 **tablespoon unsalted butter**

2 **medium onions (about 8 ounces), peeled and sliced**

¾ **pound raw potatoes, peeled and thinly sliced, or 2 medium boiled potatoes, peeled and thinly sliced**

6 **large eggs**

⅓ **cup coarsely chopped fresh chives**

½ **teaspoon salt**

¼ **teaspoon freshly ground black pepper**

1 **tomato (about 8 ounces), cut into thin slices**

1 Heat the oil and butter in a nonstick skillet until hot but not smoking. Add the onions and potatoes, and cook, covered, for about 10 minutes if using raw potatoes or 5 minutes if using cooked potatoes, stirring occasionally.

2 Meanwhile, break the eggs into a bowl. Add the chives, salt, and pepper, and mix together with a fork. Reserve.

3 Add the tomato slices to the skillet, arranging them so they cover most of the surface of the potato and onion mixture. Cover, and cook for 1 minute.

4 Preheat the broiler.

5 Add the egg mixture to the skillet, and stir gently with the tines of a fork for about 1 minute to allow the eggs to flow between the potatoes. Then place the skillet under the broiler, about 3 to 4 inches from the heat, and cook for about 3 minutes, until the eggs are set.

6 Invert onto a platter, cut into wedges, and serve.

TOTAL TIME
20 minutes

YIELD
4 servings

NUTRITIONAL ANALYSIS PER SERVING
Calories 265.1
Protein 11.9 gm.
Carbohydrates 19.6 gm.
Fat 15.8 gm.
Saturated fat 4.5 gm.
Cholesterol 326.5 mg.
Sodium 379.0 mg.

Banana Fritters

The nearer to serving time you cook the fritters, the better; they emerge from the oil crunchy and crusty, thanks to the addition of ice water, which makes the fritter batter resemble a tempura batter. If you must cook the fritters ahead, drain them on a rack, as they are here, when removed from the hot oil; then, either serve them at room temperature or place them under the broiler for a few minutes to rewarm and recrisp them. Dust the fritters with sugar just before serving.

TOTAL TIME
20 minutes

YIELD
4 servings

NUTRITIONAL ANALYSIS PER SERVING

Calories 340.7
Protein 4.6 gm.
Carbohydrates 47.9 gm.
Fat 15.4 gm.
Saturated fat 1.5 gm.
Cholesterol 53.1 mg.
Sodium 16.9 mg.

¾ **cup all-purpose flour**

1 **egg, lightly beaten**

1 **cup ice water**

About 1 cup canola oil, for frying

2 **ripe bananas**

About ⅓ cup granulated or confectioners' sugar, for dusting

1 Place the flour, egg, and about half the water in a bowl. Mix with a whisk for a few seconds, until the mixture is smooth. Whisk in the remainder of the water. If not completing the recipe immediately, refrigerate the batter until you are ready to cook the fritters.

2 To cook the fritters: In a large, nonstick skillet, heat ¼ cup of the oil to about 400 degrees. Meanwhile, peel the bananas, and, holding them directly over the bowl containing the batter, cut them crosswise into ¼-inch slices, and let the slices fall into the batter.

3 Make 3 or 4 fritters at a time, using about ¼ cup of the batter for each, and pouring it into the hot oil. Spread the mixture lightly as it hits the pan to create fritters about 3 inches in diameter. Cook for 2 to 3 minutes, turn, and cook for 2 to 3 minutes on the other side, until nicely browned.

4 Remove the fritters with a slotted spoon, and place them on a wire rack to drain. Continue to make fritters, adding more oil as needed, until all the batter has been used. Sprinkle the drained fritters generously with sugar, and serve as soon as possible.

Cooking for One

Mock Caesar Salad

Spicy Ginger and Lemon Chicken

Broccoli and Rice "Étuvée"

Pears and Roasted Nuts

Jacques 96

A s Claudine has pointed out to me, it is not easy to buy and cook for one. Many cooks find it difficult to divide recipes and scale them down to just one serving. For most of the recipes in this book, my advice is to prepare the full four servings of dishes that keep well, then freeze the extra servings for later use. In this menu, however, each recipe is designed for one.

CLAUDINE:

~

"My father's philosophy on food is to keep things as simple as they can be. Keep things simple, healthy, and good."

More often than not when I am dining alone at home, my dinner menu is decided after a thorough investigation and inventory of the contents of the refrigerator. I am always amazed to find out how many everyday "leftovers" can be transformed into wonderful dishes with just a little bit of imagination.

This is certainly the case today with the mock Caesar salad that is our first course. It is a perfect example of an inspired dish created from ordinary ingredients found in most refrigerators. Conventionally, this classic salad includes a raw egg; however, it's omitted in this version because of increased concern over possible salmonella contamination, and because a whole egg would be too much for a salad serving only one person.

The spicy chicken main course could easily be doubled for two servings or quadrupled for four servings, since this type of dish reheats well after being refrigerated or frozen.

The rice and broccoli are cooked and served together directly from the cooking vessel for an easy side dish. For dessert, nuts roasted in their shells~to enhance their flavor and keep them from getting rancid for weeks~mate beautifully with fresh pears.

As a last-minute addition to this menu, Claudine and I prepared an old family favorite, *fromage fort*. You don't need a recipe for this delightful cheese concoction. Using your food processor, simply process whatever tidbits of cheese~from blue cheese to Cheddar, Swiss, or mozzarella~you have in your refrigerator with garlic to taste and enough white wine to make the mixture creamy. Serve on toast, bread, or crackers as an appetizer or salad accompaniment.

WINE

RED

Canepa, Maipo Valley,
Cabernet Sauvignon

Mock Caesar Salad

This salad is an ideal vehicle for leftover salad greens, bread—which we turn into croutons—and cheese. Blue cheese is the standard choice for Caesar salads, but I also include some Cheddar and Camembert that I had on hand.

Although Caesar salads usually are made with romaine lettuce, I use escarole in my version, and you can substitute any other salad green varieties you have on hand. In keeping with tradition, lemon juice replaces vinegar in the dressing, which also includes garlic, olive or peanut oil, seasonings, and the crumbled cheese.

TOTAL TIME
15 minutes

YIELD
1 serving

NUTRITIONAL ANALYSIS PER SERVING
Calories 347.5
Protein 8.6 gm.
Carbohydrates 19.9 gm.
Fat 26.6 gm.
Saturated fat 5.8 gm.
Cholesterol 14.9 mg.
Sodium 709.0 mg.

2   **cups loosely packed escarole**

1   **slice stale bread (about 1 ounce)**

1½   **teaspoons canola or peanut oil**

DRESSING

½   **clove garlic, peeled**

1   **anchovy fillet in oil, coarsely chopped**

2   **teaspoons fresh lemon juice**

1   **tablespoon olive or peanut oil**

Dash salt

Dash freshly ground black pepper

2   **tablespoons crumbled blue cheese, or a combination of blue with pieces of Cheddar, Camembert, etc.**

1   Preheat the oven to 400 degrees.

2   Remove and discard any wilted or damaged areas from the salad leaves, and break the trimmed greens into 2-inch pieces. Wash the greens, and dry them thoroughly in a salad spinner.

3   Brush both sides of the bread slice with the oil, and place it on a small baking sheet. Place in the 400-degree oven for 10 minutes, or until nicely browned on both sides. Break or cut the toasted bread into 1-inch pieces.

4   Mash the garlic clove with the tines of a fork into a coarse puree. Combine it in a small bowl with the chopped anchovy, lemon juice, olive oil, salt, and pepper.

5   No more than 30 minutes before serving time, add the salad greens to the dressing in the bowl, and toss well. Sprinkle with the croutons and cheese, and serve immediately.

Spicy Ginger and Lemon Chicken

This wonderful chicken dish is made with one chicken leg that is skinned and then cooked with a uniquely flavored sweet and spicy mixture that is especially complementary with the chicken. The dish can be made ahead and reheated at serving time.

1 teaspoon virgin olive oil

1 chicken leg (8 to 10 ounces), with skin, back bones, and tips of drumsticks removed (about 6 ounces, trimmed weight)

Dash salt

⅛ teaspoon chili powder

⅛ teaspoon cumin powder

Dash dried thyme leaves

Dash cayenne pepper

½ teaspoon all-purpose flour

1 strip lemon peel, removed with a vegetable peeler

1 strip orange peel, removed with a vegetable peeler

1 teaspoon chopped fresh ginger (washed, but not peeled)

1 small clove garlic, peeled

¼ cup sweet apple cider

¼ cup water

1 Heat the oil in a large saucepan until it is hot but not smoking. Add the chicken leg, and brown it over medium heat, turning occasionally, for 10 to 12 minutes.

2 Add the rest of the ingredients, bring the mixture to a boil, reduce the heat to low, cover, and cook gently for 15 minutes. Serve with the natural cooking juices.

TOTAL TIME
35 minutes

YIELD
1 serving

NUTRITIONAL ANALYSIS PER SERVING

Calories 221.1
Protein 23.7 gm.
Carbohydrates 10.0 gm.
Fat 9.1 gm.
Saturated fat 1.7 gm.
Cholesterol 92.5 mg.
Sodium 237.5 mg.

Broccoli and Rice *Etuvée*

Served here as an accompaniment to the chicken, this also makes a good meatless main dish. I use brown rice, cooking it slowly, covered, on top of the stove until soupy; then I place the broccoli on top of the rice, cover it again, and cook it until both the rice and broccoli are tender. Not only is this combination delicious, but with only one pan involved, the cooking and cleanup are simplified. Other green vegetables could be substituted here; if you don't like broccoli, cook squash, asparagus, or green beans with the rice in the same manner.

1   teaspoon peanut or cottonseed oil

3   tablespoons chopped onion

⅓   cup short brown rice (1½ ounces)

1   cup chicken or beef stock, preferably homemade unsalted and defatted

Salt to taste

Dash red pepper flakes

1   stalk broccoli (3 to 4 ounces)

2   tablespoons grated Swiss cheese

1   Heat the oil in a small, sturdy saucepan. When it is hot, add the onion, and cook over medium heat for 2 minutes, stirring occasionally, until lightly browned.

2   Add the rice, stir well, then add the stock, salt, and red pepper flakes. Bring the mixture to a boil, cover, reduce the heat to very low, and cook for 30 minutes.

3   Meanwhile, peel the broccoli stem to remove the fibrous skin. Cut the peeled stem into ½-inch pieces and the flowerets into 1-inch pieces.

4   When the rice has cooked for 30 minutes (it will still be soupy), place the broccoli on top of the rice (don't stir it in). Cover and cook over low heat for 10 minutes. Add the grated cheese, stir, and serve immediately.

TOTAL TIME
About 55 minutes

YIELD
1 serving

NUTRITIONAL ANALYSIS PER SERVING
Calories 308.5
Protein 12.5 gm.
Carbohydrates 41.5 gm.
Fat 11.1 gm.
Saturated fat 4.1 gm.
Cholesterol 15.9 mg.
Sodium 274.2 mg.

Pears and Roasted Nuts

We finish with a simple dessert of fresh pears and roasted nuts. Mixed nuts in their shells are a favorite dessert at my house in the winter. The flavor of roasted nuts is much more intense than that of unroasted nuts, and this freshly roasted flavor is preserved so long as the nuts remain in the shells. We crack the nuts right at the table and consume them with raw pears.

TOTAL TIME
About 45 minutes

YIELD
1 serving

NUTRITIONAL ANALYSIS PER SERVING
Calories 248.4
Protein 4.2 gm.
Carbohydrates 26.3 gm.
Fat 16.4 gm.
Saturated fat 1.4 gm.
Cholesterol 0 mg.
Sodium 2.6 mg.

1 **cup unshelled mixed nuts (walnuts, pecans, hazelnuts, and almonds)**

1 **small ripe Anjou or Bosc pear (5 to 6 ounces)**

1 Preheat the oven to 375 degrees.

2 Spread the unshelled nuts on a cookie sheet, and place them in the 375-degree oven. Roast for 20 minutes, remove, and let cool for at least 30 minutes.

3 At serving time, arrange the nuts (after first cracking the shells a little, if you desire) in a basket, and place them in the center of the table with a nutcracker.

4 Peel the pear or leave it unpeeled. Cut the pear in half lengthwise, crack open some of the nuts, and eat the pear and nuts together.

A Lesson in Economy

❀

Hard-Cooked eggs in Mustard sce.

❀

Turkey Roulade "en Cocotte"

❀

Carrot and Parsley Salad

❀

Old-fashioned rice pudding with dried fruit

❀

Jacques 96

*"In Boston, I shop
at the Haymarket,
which is where
chefs buy their
produce. You get
bulk stuff—not
necessarily that
beautiful, but it
tastes good—and
you have to buy in
quantity. I'll spend
$20 and have a ton
of food. My father
and I agree, people
should definitely
not go to the market
when they are
hungry, because
they'll come home
with seven times
more food than
they can use!"*

Economy in the kitchen is the mark of a good cook, whether professional or not. A good understanding of how to manage a kitchen and use ingredients to their fullest is the greatest asset a cook can have.

The first course is hard-cooked eggs in a mustard sauce. Although people tend to avoid eggs these days because of concerns about cholesterol, when they are served only occasionally and in moderation (one per person) as they are here, eggs are an almost complete food and one of the best possible sources of protein.

Our *piéce de résistance* in this menu is a turkey roulade, which is made of a boned, stuffed, and rolled turkey leg.

Since the turkey is a substantial main course, a simple carrot and parsley salad suffices as a side dish.

An old-fashioned rice pudding provides a hearty conclusion to this meal. Flavored with dried fruit, the pudding can be made less rich if you substitute skim milk for the whole milk.

W I N E

R E D

Senda Galiana Crianza, Rioja

W H I T E

Réserve St. Martin Marsanne

Turkey Roulade *en Cocotte*

Ordinarily, the turkey skin would be used to hold the boned, stuffed meat together, but in this recipe it's removed from the leg because it contains most of the fat. Instead, the meat is rolled, wrapped, and cooked in a layer of plastic wrap and aluminum foil, which holds the roulade together and keeps it moist.

Serve the roulade in 1½-inch thick slices, or cut it into thinner slices and serve several per person. Cold roulade—either with my stuffing or one of yours—is excellent sliced and served with mustard, pickles, and a green salad.

TOTAL TIME
About 2½ hours

YIELD
4 servings

NUTRITIONAL ANALYSIS PER SERVING

Calories 544.3
Protein 44.5 gm.
Carbohydrates 36.3 gm.
Fat 20.8 gm.
Saturated fat 7.1 gm.
Cholesterol 220.2 mg.
Sodium 1,068.3 mg.

1 turkey leg (about 2½ pounds)
½ teaspoon salt
½ teaspoon freshly ground black pepper

STUFFING

5 ounces seasoned sausage meat (hot or mild)
1 bunch scallions (8 to 10), washed, trimmed, and cut into ¼-inch pieces (¾ cup)
6 dried figs (4 ounces), cut into ¼-inch pieces (¾ cup), or a like amount of another dried fruit
1 egg
2 ounces whole wheat bread, about 2 days old, processed into coarse crumbs in a food processor (1¾ cups)

SAUCE

1 tomato (10 ounces), cut into 1-inch pieces
1 medium onion (6 ounces), peeled and cut into 1-inch pieces
6 cloves garlic, unpeeled
1 tablespoon dark soy sauce
1 cup dry, fruity white wine
1 teaspoon *herbes de Provence*

1 Cut off the tip of the drumstick with a cleaver. Using a dish towel, pull the skin from the leg. Cut alongside the thigh and drumstick bones and around the knee joint, then remove the bones. (Skinned and boned, the meat will weigh about 1½ pounds. The bones will weigh about 8 ounces and the skin

about 4 ounces.) Discard the skin, and reserve the bones.

2 Using pliers, pull out as many sinews from the drumstick as you can see. (Do not worry if some still remain.) Add the sinews to the bones. Sprinkle the meat on both sides with the salt and pepper, and place it, skin side down, in the center of a 12-inch square of plastic wrap.

3 *For the stuffing:* Mix the sausage meat in a bowl with the scallions, figs, and egg until well combined. Add the bread crumbs, and mix just enough to combine lightly.

4 Arrange the stuffing on top of the meat and, using the plastic wrap, wrap the meat around it as best you can. The meat may not wrap completely around the stuffing, but make it as tight as possible with the plastic wrap, then twist the wrap at either end. Place the roll in the center of a 12-inch square of aluminum foil, and wrap the foil around it tightly, twisting the foil at both ends to make a roulade that is about 9 inches long by 3 inches thick.

5 Place the roulade in the center of a heavy casserole (an enameled

cast iron pot is good), and arrange the bones, sinews, tomato, onion, garlic, soy sauce, wine, and *herbes de Provence* around it. Bring the mixture to a boil, uncovered, over high heat, then reduce the heat to low, and cook gently for 1½ hours. Transfer the roulade to a plate, and set it aside.

6 *For the sauce:* Remove and discard the bones and sinews. Push the remaining solids and the liquid through a food mill. (You should have about 2 cups.) Using an immersible hand blender, emulsify the mixture to make it creamy.

7 Return the sauce to the casserole. Unwrap the roulade, removing both the foil and the plastic wrap. Using pliers, pull out any sinews you did not remove earlier. (They will pull out easily from the cooked meat.)

8 Place the roulade, seam side down, in the sauce. Bring the sauce back to a boil over high heat, then reduce the heat to very low, and simmer gently, covered, for 15 minutes.

9 Let the roulade rest for 15 minutes in the sauce, then slice, and serve with the sauce.

Hard-Cooked Eggs in Mustard Sauce

I am very finicky about my cooked eggs. I want them cooked very gently in boiling water to prevent the white—mostly albumen—from toughening, and then they should be refreshed immediately in ice water. I like the yolks yellow throughout, with their centers slightly soft.

The eggs should be left until completely cool in the ice water so that the sulfur in them—the element responsible for giving eggs an unappealing odor and turning the outer part of the yolks green—has enough time to be extracted and dissipate in the water. The sauce accompaniment is a vinaigrette containing a lot of mustard, a perfect combination with the eggs.

TOTAL TIME
15 minutes

YIELD
4 servings

NUTRITIONAL ANALYSIS PER SERVING

Calories 173.2
Protein 6.5 gm.
Carbohydrates 1.6 gm.
Fat 15.3 gm.
Saturated fat 2.3 gm.
Cholesterol 212.5 mg.
Sodium 223.8 mg.

4 **large eggs**

MUSTARD SAUCE

1 **large clove garlic, peeled, crushed, and chopped (1 teaspoon)**

1 **tablespoon Dijon-style mustard**

⅛ **teaspoon freshly ground black pepper**

⅛ **teaspoon salt**

2 **teaspoons wine vinegar**

3 **tablespoons canola or safflower oil**

8 **lettuce leaves, rinsed and dried**

1 **tablespoon chopped fresh chives**

Crusty French bread

1 Bring 2 cups of water to a boil in a saucepan. Using a thumbtack or pushpin, make a small hole in the rounded end of each egg. Lower the eggs gently into the boiling water. Bring the water back to a very gentle boil, and cook the eggs for 8 to 9 minutes. Drain off the water, and shake the pan to crack the shells of the eggs. Then add ice to the pan, and let the eggs cool completely.

2 Meanwhile, make the mustard sauce: Combine all the sauce ingredients except the oil in a bowl. Add the oil slowly, mixing it in with a whisk or a spoon as it is added. Set aside at room temperature until ready to use. Do not worry if the sauce separates.

3 Shell the eggs, and cut them in half lengthwise. The centers of the yolks should be slightly soft. Divide the lettuce leaves among four plates, and place 2 egg halves cut side up on top of the lettuce on each plate. Coat the eggs with the mustard sauce, sprinkle with chives, and serve immediately with crusty French bread.

Carrot and Parsley Salad

This carrot and parsley salad appears often on my table. The carrots can be grated by hand or in a food processor fitted with a shredding insert. I use lots of parsley and garlic, and I season the salad with a simple oil and vinegar dressing for a fresh flavor.

¾ **pound carrots, peeled and shredded into small strands on a hand grater (large holes) or in a food processor fitted with the shredding insert (2½ cups)**

1¼ **cups flat-leaf parsley leaves, rinsed and dried**

2 **large cloves garlic, peeled, crushed, and finely chopped (1½ teaspoons)**

½ **teaspoon salt**

¼ **teaspoon freshly ground black pepper**

4 **teaspoons red wine or cider vinegar**

3 **tablespoons peanut or safflower oil**

1 Place the shredded carrots, parsley leaves, and chopped garlic in a bowl. Stir in the remaining ingredients, and mix well. Serve.

TOTAL TIME
About 15 minutes

YIELD
4 servings

NUTRITIONAL ANALYSIS PER SERVING

Calories 131.6
Protein 1.3 gm.
Carbohydrates 9.7 gm.
Fat 10.3 gm.
Saturated fat 1.7 gm.
Cholesterol 0 mg.
Sodium 307.7 mg.

Old-fashioned Rice Pudding with Dried Fruit

Notice that the proportion of liquid to rice is quite high here, so you end up with a creamy, almost soupy, mixture that is not at all like the tight, pasty rice pudding you may have encountered as a child. I add dried fruit—raisins, apricots, apples, and figs—to my pudding, but you can eliminate any of these that are not to your liking. If you are counting calories, top the pudding with yogurt instead of sour cream, or serve it plain—without any topping.

TOTAL TIME
45 minutes, plus cooling time

YIELD
4 servings

NUTRITIONAL ANALYSIS PER SERVING
Calories 371.6
Protein 10.4 gm.
Carbohydrates 64.9 gm.
Fat 8.5 gm.
Saturated fat 5.1 gm.
Cholesterol 34.2 mg.
Sodium 126.8 mg.

- **4 cups whole or skim milk**
- **⅓ cup sugar**
- **1½ teaspoons vanilla extract**
- **½ cup long-grain white rice**
- **1 teaspoon grated lemon rind**
- **¾ cup diced (½-inch) dried fruits (raisins, apricots, figs, apples, etc.)**
- **¾ cup yogurt or sour cream (optional)**

1 Bring the milk, sugar, and vanilla to a boil in a saucepan. Add the rice, mix well, and bring the mixture back to a boil. Cover, reduce the heat to very low, and simmer for about 40 minutes, until the rice is very soft. (The mixture should still be soupy at this point; if it is not, add enough additional milk to make it soupy.)

2 Add the lemon rind and dried fruits to the pudding, mix, and set aside until cooled to room temperature.

3 Spoon into four dessert dishes and serve, if desired, with 1 or 2 tablespoons of yogurt or sour cream on top.

Eggplant Cushions

Sea Bass in Potato Crust

Curried Cole Slaw

Melon and Strawberries
in
Honey Sauce

The Sorcerer's Apprentice

After a few weeks of instruction, Claudine prepared this meal for us. Simple and delicious, it demonstrated what patience and practice can accomplish in the kitchen.

The flavorful first course consists of thick slabs of eggplant that are baked, then topped with herbs-and-garlic-flavored bread crumbs and broiled before serving.

The main course features sea bass, a fish long appreciated by Oriental cooks for its firm, moist, delicate texture. Select small individual fillets, each about 6 ounces, for this dish, and begin by removing any bones or sinews.

The sea bass fillets are served in a potato crust. Each fillet is pushed into a small mound of shredded potatoes and chopped leeks, and then covered with more of the potato mixture. As these "packages" cook in the skillet, the fillets remain tender and moist while the potatoes surrounding them become brown and crusty.

A refreshing curried cole slaw complements our main course, although it could be served as a first course as well.

To complete our meal, a melon and strawberry dessert, particularly appealing in late spring and summer, when these fruits are at their flavor peak, is served. The dessert can be made a few hours ahead and refrigerated. If you do so, however, remove the fruit at least 45 minutes before serving, since it is more flavorful served cool rather than cold.

WINES

WHITE

Chassagne Montrachet

PORT

Chateau Reynella,
Old Cave Tawny Port

Eggplant Cushions

For this dish, thick slices of eggplant are lightly coated with oil on both sides, then baked in one layer on a baking sheet until soft. Cooked this way, the slices absorb only about a quarter as much oil as they would if fried in a skillet.

The slices can be baked ahead, but should be finished under the broiler at the last minute. For finishing, cubes of leftover bread are processed with some garlic, herbs, and olive oil in a food processor, then the crumbed mixture is piled atop the eggplant slices, and they are broiled until the eggplant is hot and the topping nicely browned. Although served as a first course here, this dish also makes a good accompaniment to meat or fish.

TOTAL TIME
About 45 minutes

YIELD
4 servings

NUTRITIONAL ANALYSIS PER SERVING

Calories 138.3
Protein 2.8 gm.
Carbohydrates 16.0 gm.
Fat 7.8 gm.
Saturated fat 0.8 gm.
Cholesterol 0 mg.
Sodium 483.9 mg.

2 eggplants (about 1¾ pounds total), each about 3 to 4 inches in diameter

1½ tablespoons canola oil

¾ teaspoon salt

1½ ounces leftover bread, preferably from a baguette, cut into 1-inch pieces

¼ cup mixture chopped fresh chives and fresh parsley

1 clove garlic, peeled

2 teaspoons virgin olive oil

1 Preheat the oven to 400 degrees.

2 Trim the eggplants, peel them, and cut them into thick slices, each about 1 1/4 inches thick. You should have about 8 slices.

3 Pour the canola oil on a large baking sheet, spreading it evenly. Press the eggplant slices in the oil, and sprinkle them with half the salt. Turn the slices over, arrange them in one layer on the sheet, and sprinkle them with the remaining salt.

4 Bake the eggplant slices in the 400-degree oven for 30 minutes, or until the eggplant flesh is very soft.

5 Meanwhile, place the bread cubes, herbs, and garlic in the bowl of a food processor, and process for 15 to 20 seconds. Transfer the crumbled mixture to a bowl and toss it lightly with the olive oil. Once the eggplant slices are removed from the oven, spoon the crumbs on top of them.

6 About 10 minutes before serving time, preheat a broiler.

7 Place the eggplant slices so that the stuffing on top is at least 6 to 8 inches from the heat. Broil for 5 to 6 minutes, until the topping is nicely browned. Serve immediately.

Curried Cole Slaw

A dash of curry is added to this cole slaw to give it an interesting tang. An invigorating dish, it is the perfect accompaniment for our sea bass and potato main course.

1 **small head cabbage or half a larger head (1¼ pounds)**

1 **carrot (4 ounces), peeled**

⅓ **cup mayonnaise**

3 **tablespoons cider vinegar**

1 **tablespoon sugar**

1 **teaspoon salt**

2 **teaspoons poppy seeds**

¼ **teaspoon Tabasco hot pepper sauce**

1 **teaspoon curry powder**

1 Trim the cabbage, removing and discarding any damaged parts, and shred it on a slicer or by cutting it into thin slices with a sharp knife. (You should have 5 to 6 lightly packed cups of cabbage.) Shred the carrot. (You should have 1 lightly packed cup.)

2 In a bowl large enough to hold the finished cole slaw, mix together the mayonnaise, vinegar, sugar, salt, poppy seeds, Tabasco, and curry powder. Add the cabbage and carrots, and mix well. Serve immediately, or cover, refrigerate, and serve later. The cole slaw will keep, refrigerated, for up to one day.

TOTAL TIME
10 to 15 minutes

YIELD
4 servings

NUTRITIONAL ANALYSIS PER SERVING

Calories 198.2
Protein 2.5 gm.
Carbohydrates 15.1 gm.
Fat 15.4 gm.
Saturated fat 2.2 gm.
Cholesterol 10.7 mg.
Sodium 690.5 mg.

Sea Bass in Potato Crust

For this recipe, sea bass fillets are cooked in a potato crust. Use large baking potatoes, first peeling them (although they can be left unpeeled, if you prefer) and washing them, then shredding them against the side of a cheese grater with the largest holes. At this point, the potatoes should be used immediately or kept in water to cover until ready to cook.

TOTAL TIME
30 to 35 minutes

YIELD
4 servings

NUTRITIONAL ANALYSIS PER SERVING
Calories 289.7
Protein 29.0 gm.
Carbohydrates 21.8 gm.
Fat 9.3 gm.
Saturated fat 3.4 gm.
Cholesterol 65.9 mg.
Sodium 382.5 mg.

4   **fillets of sea bass (about 1½ pounds)**

2   **large Idaho potatoes (1 pound total)**

½   **medium leek (about 3 ounces), washed and finely chopped (½ cup)**

1   **tablespoon cottonseed or safflower oil**

1   **tablespoon unsalted butter**

½   **teaspoon salt**

1   Remove and discard any bones or sinews from the fillets. When cleaned, each fillet should weigh about 5 ounces.

2   Peel the potatoes (or leave them unpeeled, if desired), and wash them. Using the side of a cheese grater with the large holes, shred the potatoes. (You should have about 2½ cups.) Drain well in a colander, then place in a bowl with the leek. Mix well.

3   At cooking time, place the oil and butter in a large skillet, preferably nonstick, and heat until hot. Meanwhile, sprinkle half the salt on the fillets.

4   When the oil and butter are hot, place four, small, evenly spaced mounds of the shredded potatoes and leek (each about ⅓ cup) in the skillet. Press a portion of fish into each mound, and cover the fish with the remaining potatoes. Sprinkle with the remaining salt.

5   Cook the potato packages over medium to high heat, uncovered, for 6 to 7 minutes. Turn them carefully with a large spatula, and cook them for an additional 6 to 7 minutes on the other side. The potatoes should be nicely crusted on both sides and the fish inside lightly cooked. Serve immediately.

Melon and Strawberries in Honey Sauce

When selecting cantaloupes, your nose is the best indicator of ripeness. Choose a melon with a sweet, fruity fragrance.

TOTAL TIME
15 minutes

YIELD
4 servings

NUTRITIONAL ANALYSIS PER SERVING

Calories 107.3
Protein 1.1 gm.
Carbohydrates 27.7 gm.
Fat 0.4 gm.
Saturated fat 0 gm.
Cholesterol 0 mg.
Sodium 9.0 mg.

¼ cup honey

1 tablespoon grated orange rind

2 to 3 tablespoons orange juice

1 tablespoon Grand Marnier

1 large cantaloupe (about 1½ pounds), seeded, peeled, and cut into 1-inch pieces (2½ cups)

1 cup strawberries, washed, hulled, and halved or quartered, depending on size (about ¾ cup)

1 Combine the honey, orange rind, orange juice, and Grand Marnier in a bowl large enough to hold the melon and strawberries. Add both fruits, and toss thoroughly.

2 Refrigerate until serving time. (This dessert can be assembled up to 6 hours ahead.)

3 At serving time, divide the fruit mixture among four goblets.

Basic Techniques from a Pro

Weekly Planner

Leg of Lamb

Scotch Barley and Mushroom Soup

Curry of Lamb

Lamb Steaks in Vinegar Sauce

Lamb Roast

Gratin Dauphinois

Although a leg of lamb is excellent roasted whole for a large party or family gathering, it is my goal here to show that many recipes can be created from this same cut of meat.

This assemblage of dishes is not a menu but a session and a lesson on lamb. It is intended to teach Claudine and other less experienced home cooks about economy and proper planning in the kitchen.

Divided as it is here, a leg of lamb will yield more than twenty diversified main-course portions. The bones are used for soup, the less tender pieces of leg meat for a curried stew, the top round for steaks, and the top sirloin and top knuckle for a roast. Using the leg in this way makes it an extremely economical purchase and reflects a process that is essential in a well-run kitchen.

WINES

RED

Stonestreet, Merlot

Château Larose-Trintaudon, Haut-Médoc

The creamy, garlic-flavored gratin known as gratin *dauphinois* is a side dish that works particularly well with lamb, especially the roast and the steaks. The curry would be better served with plain boiled rice, noodles, or potatoes.

Starting the Menu: Leg of Lamb

1 leg of lamb, bone in, about 9½ pounds

Trim off all fat, bone out, and divide into these parts:

1½ pounds fat, to be discarded

2 pounds bones, for use in Scotch Barley and Mushroom Soup (page 58)

2¾ pounds lamb meat, for use in Curry of Lamb (page 59)

1¼ pounds top round, cut into 4 steaks, for use in Lamb Steaks in Vinegar Sauce (page 61)

1 piece of top sirloin (about 12 ounces) and 1 piece of top knuckle (about 20 ounces), for use in Lamb Roast (page 62)

CLAUDINE:

~

"I think that if anybody ever gave me a leg of lamb, I'd call my father and have the knife available, right there, so he could instruct me over the phone. Or else I'd trot it back to the butcher and say, 'Excuse me, could you divide this just like Jacques Pépin does on TV?'— and hope he doesn't recognize me."

Scotch Barley and Mushroom Soup

This is one of those hearty winter soups that makes a great dinner entrée when accompanied by crusty bread and followed by a green salad and a piece of cheese. In addition, it can be served in smaller portions as a first course when followed by an unadorned fish or simple grilled meat main dish. If you chill or freeze the soup for later use, it is best to reheat it in a double boiler, since it tends to stick.

TOTAL TIME
2½ hours

YIELD
3 quarts; serves 6 to 8 as a main course, 10 to 12 as a first course

NUTRITIONAL ANALYSIS PER SERVING
Calories 107.4
Protein 4.7 gm.
Carbohydrates 20.4 gm.
Fat 1.4 gm.
Saturated fat 0.5 gm.
Cholesterol 2.5 mg.
Sodium 649.9 mg.

2 **pounds lamb bones**

3 **quarts cold water**

7 **ounces pearl barley (1 cup)**

1 **tablespoon salt**

1 **cup diced (½-inch) celery**

8 **ounces mushrooms, washed and cut into ½-inch dice (3 cups)**

1 **large leek (8 ounces), washed and cut into ½-inch dice (3 cups)**

2 **carrots (8 ounces), peeled and cut into ½-inch dice (1½ cups)**

1 **white turnip (8 ounces), peeled and cut into ½-inch dice (1½ cups)**

1 Place the bones in a large kettle with the cold water. Bring to a boil, and boil gently, uncovered, for 20 minutes. Skim off and discard the scum and fat from the surface of the liquid.

2 Add the barley and salt, mix well, and bring the liquid back to a boil over high heat. Then reduce the heat to very low, cover, and cook for 1 hour. Remove the bones, and set them aside to cool.

3 Add all the vegetables to the pot, and bring the liquid back to a boil over high heat. Reduce the heat to very low, cover, and cook gently for 20 minutes.

4 When the bones are cool enough to handle, remove any pieces of meat attached to them, and cut it into ½-inch pieces. (My bones yielded 1½ cups of meat.) Add the meat to the soup while the vegetables are cooking.

5 Serve immediately, or cool and freeze or refrigerate for later use. Refrigerated soup will keep for 3 to 4 days. If soup is too thick when reheating, dilute to desired consistency with water.

Curry of Lamb

Lamb curry is an excellent concoction, especially appealing to people who like spicy food—although the hotness can be controlled and adjusted to suit individual taste preferences. Most people do not realize how easy it is to make a stew; this recipe, for example, involves only a few minutes of work. It will keep for 5 or 6 days in the refrigerator, or it can be frozen.

1	tablespoon canola or peanut oil
2¾	pounds lamb pieces from the leg, cut into 1½- to 2-inch pieces
1	medium onion (6 ounces), peeled and coarsely chopped (1¼ cups)
2	medium apples (about 10 ounces), left unpeeled, cored, and cut into ½-inch pieces (2½ cups)
1	banana (6 ounces), peeled and sliced (¾ cup)
2	bay leaves
¼	cup curry powder
1	teaspoon cumin powder
1	teaspoon allspice powder
1½	teaspoons salt
2	tablespoons tomato paste
2	cups water
2	tablespoons chopped fresh parsley
	Chutney (optional)

1 Heat the oil in a sturdy pot (enameled cast iron is good). When it is hot, add the lamb (it will take up more than one layer). Cook, uncovered, over high heat, stirring occasionally, until the liquid emerging from the lamb has evaporated, and the lamb is sizzling nicely, about 10 to 12 minutes.

2 Add all the remaining ingredients except the parsley and chutney, and mix well. Bring to a boil over high heat, uncovered, then reduce the heat to very low, cover, and cook for 1¼ hours, stirring occasionally to prevent the mixture from sticking to the bottom of the pot. Remove and discard the bay leaves.

3 Sprinkle with the parsley, and serve with rice, noodles, or potatoes. Pass some chutney, if desired.

TOTAL TIME
1 hour 45 minutes

YIELD
6 servings

NUTRITIONAL ANALYSIS PER SERVING

Calories 360.5
Protein 44.2 gm.
Carbohydrates 17.3 gm.
Fat 12.7 gm.
Saturated fat 3.6 gm.
Cholesterol 133.2 mg.
Sodium 725.7 mg.

Lamb Steaks in Vinegar Sauce

This quick, elegant recipe is ideal for a special dinner. Conventionally, reduced brown stock or demi-glace is used to create a sauce, but I substitute a piquant mixture of ketchup, soy sauce, vinegar, and chili sauce. Fresh noodles or basmati rice would make a nice accompaniment, as would sautéed or roasted potatoes or Gratin *Dauphinois* (page 64).

1 tablespoon unsalted butter

1 tablespoon canola oil

4 lamb steaks, each 5 ounces and about 1 inch thick

¼ teaspoon salt

¼ teaspoon freshly ground black pepper

3 cloves garlic, peeled, crushed, and chopped (2 teaspoons)

¼ cup balsamic vinegar

½ cup water

2 tablespoons ketchup

1 teaspoon soy sauce

1 teaspoon chili sauce with garlic (optional)

1 tablespoon shredded fresh mint

1 Preheat the oven to 170 degrees.

2 Heat the butter and oil in a skillet large enough to hold the lamb steaks in one layer. Sprinkle the steaks with the salt and pepper, and sauté them in the skillet over high heat for about 2 minutes a side. Remove the steaks, placing them on a tray or ovenproof plate. Keep warm in the 170-degree oven while you make the sauce.

3 Add the garlic to the drippings in the skillet, and cook for 10 seconds. Add the vinegar, and cook over high heat for 1 minute, until the vinegar has evaporated. Add the water, ketchup, soy sauce, and, if desired, the chili sauce. Boil for about 30 seconds, stirring to mix in all the solidified juices.

4 At serving time, pour the juices that have accumulated around the steaks into the sauce. Arrange a steak on each of four individual plates, and coat the steaks with the sauce. Garnish with the mint.

TOTAL TIME
10 to 15 minutes

YIELD
4 servings

NUTRITIONAL ANALYSIS PER SERVING
Calories 268.4
Protein 32.4 gm.
Carbohydrates 3.3 gm.
Fat 13.3 gm.
Saturated fat 4.5 gm.
Cholesterol 107.6 mg.
Sodium 408.1 mg.

Lamb Roast

The two pieces of meat, or "muscle," chosen for this roast are the juiciest parts of the leg. Browning the pieces on top of the stove first creates a caramelized crust that gives the roast a wonderfully nutty flavor.

TOTAL TIME
30 minutes

YIELD
6 servings

NUTRITIONAL ANALYSIS PER SERVING

Calories 221.7
Protein 31.3 gm.
Carbohydrates 1.0 gm.
Fat 8.7 gm.
Saturated fat 3.6 gm.
Cholesterol 102.0 mg.
Sodium 295.6 mg.

2 pounds lamb meat from the leg (1 top sirloin and 1 top knuckle)

3 cloves garlic, peeled and cut into about 12 slivers

½ teaspoon salt

½ teaspoon freshly ground black pepper

1 teaspoon *herbes de Provence*

1 tablespoon unsalted butter

2 teaspoons Worcestershire sauce

¼ cup dry, fruity white wine

¼ cup water

1 Preheat the oven to 400 degrees.

2 Using the point of a small paring knife, make about 12 evenly spaced incisions, each about ½ inch deep, into the meat. Push a sliver of garlic into each cut. Sprinkle the meat with the salt, pepper, and *herbes de Provence*. Melt the butter in a heavy skillet (*not* nonstick).

3 Brown the 2 pieces of meat in the saucepan over medium heat for 7 to 8 minutes, turning it several times so that it browns on all sides.

4 Place the meat in the 400-degree oven, and cook about 6 minutes for the small piece of meat and 12 minutes for the large one. Remove the meat as it finishes cooking, and place it on an ovenproof platter. Reduce the oven temperature to 170 degrees (or preheat a second oven to 170 degrees), and place the meat back in the oven until serving time. (The meat should "rest" in the warm oven for at least 10 minutes but can wait as long as 45 to 60 minutes.)

5 To finish, add the Worcestershire sauce, wine, and water to the drippings in the skillet, and bring to a boil, scraping the skillet with a wooden spatula to release and melt the solidified juices.

6 Thinly slice the meat, and serve, spooning some of the juices over the slices.

G ratin *Dauphinois*

This dish is my version of a classic from my youth. My mother has always made her gratin exclusively with milk, and topped the potatoes with grated Swiss cheese before baking. I don't include cheese in my recipe, and I add a little cream. However, you can follow my mother's example and use milk only for a leaner but still delicious gratin.

It is important that the potatoes not be washed after they are sliced. Washing removes most of the starch from potatoes, but it's needed here to thicken the mixture as it comes to a boil on top of the stove before baking.

One of the greatest treats about this dish for me is in enjoying the leftovers cool or at room temperature the next day; it goes well with a salad of curly endive or escarole dressed with a mustardy garlic dressing.

TOTAL TIME
About 1 hour 40 minutes (including resting time before serving)

YIELD
6 to 8 servings as an accompaniment

NUTRITIONAL ANALYSIS PER SERVING
Calories 215.6
Protein 6.0 gm.
Carbohydrates 26.0 gm.
Fat 10.0 gm.
Saturated fat 6.1 gm.
Cholesterol 37.9 mg.
Sodium 301.9 mg.

1¾ **pounds potatoes, preferably Yukon Gold, peeled**

3 **cups milk**

2 **or 3 cloves garlic, peeled, crushed, and chopped fine (1½ teaspoons)**

¾ **teaspoon salt**

½ **teaspoon freshly ground black pepper**

½ **cup heavy cream**

1 Preheat the oven to 375 degrees.

2 Wash the peeled potatoes, and slice them by hand or with the slicing blade of a food processor into slices ⅛ inch thick. Do *not* wash the slices.

3 Place the potato slices in a saucepan with the milk, garlic, salt, and pepper. Bring to a boil, stirring gently to separate the slices and prevent the mixture from scorching. It will thicken as it reaches a boil.

4 Pour the potato mixture into a 6-cup gratin dish, and pour the cream on top. Place the dish on a cookie sheet, and bake in the 375-degree oven for 1 hour.

5 Let the potatoes rest for 20 to 30 minutes before serving.

the Pastry Lesson

Leeks and Gruyère Quiche

Monkfish and Salmon Mousse in Crust
with tomato-Butter Sauce

Raspberry Cookie Dough Galette

Jacques
96

The purpose of this demonstration is to show Claudine how to make different doughs, and then how to use them. We will work with two of the most useful doughs: a buttery, flaky pie dough and a sweet cookie-type dough.

A classic *pâte brisée*—pie dough—is transformed into a quiche with leeks and Gruyère cheese. Exhibiting its versatility, the same dough is used as the showy crust for a monkfish and salmon mousse with spinach.

The sweet dough—or *pâte sucrée*, as the French call it—is best suited for delicate desserts. Here, it's the base for a raspberry *galette*.

For many cooks, tarts, quiche, and fish in crust are too difficult and time-consuming to make for two to four servings. Therefore, the recipes in this chapter are for six to eight.

Special Tip

When measuring flour, always dip the measuring cup into the flour container and fill the cup to overflowing, then lift it out and level it off to remove the excess flour. Although it is not necessary to weigh flour for some recipes, I think it is essential when making pastry or bread. Properly measured and weighed, 3 cups of all-purpose flour will weigh 1 pound.

W I N E S

WHITE

Kendall Jackson,
Vintner's Reserve, Fumé Blanc

RED

Temple Bruer, Grenache

Leek and Gruyère Quiche

Even though many in the "gourmet" crowd consider quiche a bit passé, it is still one of the best combinations around. The filling varieties are endless—from bacon to mushrooms, from spinach to truffles. In this recipe, the dough is partially baked beforehand because the filling needs only 20 to 25 minutes to cook (that wouldn't be enough time for the dough to cook completely). Prebaking the dough in this manner is also a common practice when making fruit tarts and lemon meringue–type pies.

TOTAL TIME
About 1 hour 45 minutes, including cooling time after cooking

YIELD
6 to 8 servings

NUTRITIONAL ANALYSIS PER SERVING
Calories 348.1
Protein 12.7 gm.
Carbohydrates 23.1 gm.
Fat 22.8 gm.
Saturated fat 13.0 gm.
Cholesterol 183.6 mg.
Sodium 318.3 mg.

PÂTE BRISÉE

- 1 cup all-purpose flour (5 to 5½ ounces)
- 6 tablespoons cold unsalted butter (¾ stick), cut into ½-inch slices
- ⅛ teaspoon salt
- ¼ teaspoon sugar
- About 3 tablespoons ice water

FILLING

- 1 large or 2 small leeks (about 8 ounces), trimmed (with most of the green left on), washed, and thinly sliced (2 cups)
- ¾ cup water
- 4 large eggs
- ½ teaspoon salt
- ½ teaspoon freshly ground black pepper
- 1½ cups grated Gruyère cheese (4 ounces)
- 1¼ cups milk
- ¼ cup heavy cream

1 Preheat the oven to 400 degrees.

2 *For the dough:* Place the flour, butter, the ⅛ teaspoon salt, and the sugar in the bowl of a food processor. Pulsing the motor, process the mixture for 5 to 10 seconds, just until the butter is broken into small (but still visible) pieces. Add the 3 tablespoons ice water (you may have to add a little less or a little more, depending on the dryness of the flour), and process for 10 to 15 seconds longer. The dough may not have formed into a ball at this point; transfer it to a bowl, and press it gently together to form it into a ball.

3 Place the ball of dough in the center of a sheet of plastic wrap

about 13 inches square, and lay another piece of plastic wrap the same size on top. Roll the dough between the plastic wrap sheets to form a circle about 13 inches in diameter.

4 Remove the plastic wrap from the top of the circle of dough, and invert the dough into a 9½-×-1-inch quiche pan with a removable bottom. Before peeling the remaining sheet of plastic wrap from the dough, use it to press the dough into place in the pan. The dough should extend about ½ inch above the edge of the pan. Roll or press this overhang back on the dough at the edge to make it thicker.

5 Line the dough shell with a double-thick layer of aluminum foil, pressing the foil gently into place. (The foil should be rigid enough to hold the dough in place as it cooks.) Place the quiche pan on a cookie sheet, and bake the dough in the 400-degree oven for 20 minutes. Then carefully remove the aluminum foil, and cook the dough for another 20 to 25 minutes, until it is lightly browned inside.

6 *For the filling:* Meanwhile, place the leeks and the ¾ cup water in a saucepan, and bring the mixture to a boil over high heat. Boil, uncovered, for about 5 minutes, until the water has evaporated and the leeks are soft.

7 Beat the eggs in a bowl until smooth. Stir in the ½ teaspoon salt, pepper, cheese, milk, and cream. Mix in the leeks. (There should be about 4 cups of the filling mixture.) Reduce the oven heat to 375 degrees.

8 Pour the filling into the precooked dough in the quiche pan while it is still on the cookie sheet in the oven. (The filling will come to the brim of the shell, and there is less likelihood of its spilling if the shell is not removed from the oven.) Cook at 375 degrees for 20 to 25 minutes, until the filling is completely set and beautifully browned on top.

9 Let the quiche rest for 10 to 15 minutes before cutting it into wedges and serving.

Note: The quiche can be baked ahead and reheated, uncovered, in a 375-degree oven until warmed through.

Monkfish and Salmon Mousse in Crust with Tomato-Butter Sauce

A fish *en croûte* (in crust) is always the showstopper in a special meal—especially when the crust is shaped and decorated to resemble a fish. Although this dish can be assembled a few hours ahead, for best results it should be cooked close to serving time. You can substitute another fish for the monkfish, providing the fillet used is thick and firm, so that it holds its shape during cooking.

TOTAL TIME
1½ hours

YIELD
6 to 8 servings

NUTRITIONAL ANALYSIS PER SERVING

Calories 493.0
Protein 21.7 gm.
Carbohydrates 34.0 gm.
Fat 30.1 gm.
Saturated fat 16.8 gm.
Cholesterol 135.6 mg.
Sodium 433.9 mg.

PÂTE BRISÉE

- 2 cups all-purpose flour (10 to 10½ ounces), plus 2 tablespoons for use in rolling out dough
- 1½ sticks cold, unsalted butter (6 ounces), cut into ½-inch slices
- ⅛ teaspoon salt
- ¼ teaspoon sugar
- About ⅓ cup ice water

MOUSSE

- 6 ounces cleaned salmon fillet, cut into 1-inch pieces
- 1 egg
- ¼ cup heavy cream
- ¼ teaspoon salt
- ⅛ teaspoon freshly ground black pepper
- 1 tablespoon chopped fresh dill

FISH AND SPINACH FILLING

- 4 ounces washed and trimmed spinach leaves (4 tightly packed cups)
- 1 monkfish fillet (about 18 ounces)
- ¼ teaspoon salt
- ¼ teaspoon freshly ground black pepper

TOMATO-BUTTER SAUCE

- 2 tomatoes (12 ounces), cut into 1-inch pieces
- ½ cup tomato sauce
- ¾ cup water
- ¼ teaspoon salt
- ¼ teaspoon freshly ground black pepper
- ½ teaspoon sugar
- 2 tablespoons unsalted butter

1 *For the dough:* Place the flour, the cold butter slices, the ⅛ teaspoon salt, and the ¼ teaspoon sugar in the bowl of a food processor. Pulse the motor for about 10 seconds. Add the ⅓ cup water (you may have to add a little less or a little more, depending on the dryness of the flour) and process again, pulsing the motor, for another 10 seconds. (The mixture may not have gathered into a ball at this point.) Transfer the mixture to a bowl, and knead it for a few seconds, just enough so that it can be gathered into a ball. Set aside, wrapped in plastic wrap and refrigerated.

2 *For the mousse:* Place the salmon pieces in the bowl of a food processor. In a small mixing bowl, beat the egg with a fork. Reserving 1 tablespoon of the beaten egg for later use as a glaze, add the remainder to the food processor bowl with the salmon. Process for 10 seconds. Then, while the machine is running, add the cream, and process for another 10 seconds. Add the ¼ teaspoon salt and ⅛ teaspoon pepper, and process for 5 to 10 seconds longer. Transfer the mousse to a mixing bowl, and stir in the dill. Set aside until ready to assemble the dish.

3 *For the filling:* Place the spinach leaves (still damp from washing) in a skillet, and cook, covered, for 4 to 5 minutes over medium to high heat, until the spinach is wilted and most of the moisture has evaporated. Cool, uncovered.

4 Remove and discard the surrounding black flesh and sinews from the monkfish fillet. (The cleaned fillet should weigh about 1 pound and should be about 9 inches long by 1½ inches thick.) Butterfly the fillet lengthwise: Holding a sharp knife parallel to the fillet on the table, cut almost through the thickness of the fillet, beginning on one of the long sides and stopping just before you get to the other long side, then open the fillet like a book and lay it flat.

5 Press the cooled spinach leaves between your palms to extrude most of the remaining water, and arrange them on the butterflied fish. Sprinkle with the ¼ teaspoon each salt and pepper. Refold the fillet to enclose the filling.

(continued)

6 *To begin the assembly:* Roll the dough to form a rectangle about 12 by 18 inches. Spread half the mousse in the center of the rectangle, then arrange the spinach-filled fillet on top. Spread the remaining mousse on top of and around the fish.

7 Preheat the oven to 450 degrees.

8 Moisten the dough along one 12-inch side, then join the sides of the dough together on top, pressing gently along the seam so the overlapping edges stick together. Trim off and reserve any excess dough. Fold in the ends of the dough, leaving one end longer and molding it to resemble a fish tail. Trim off and reserve any excess dough.

9 Transfer the rolled "fish" to a lightly floured jelly roll pan so the dough seams are underneath. Use dough trimmings to mark the eyes and create fins on the fish. Use the reserved tablespoon of beaten egg to brush the top and sides of the fish. Then, using the tines of a fork, make scalelike designs on the fish.

10 Place the fish in the 450-degree oven for about 30 minutes to lightly brown the dough, then reduce the heat to 350 degrees, and cook for another 15 minutes, for a total cooking time of 45 minutes.

11 Meanwhile, *make the tomato-butter sauce:* Bring the tomatoes, tomato sauce, and ¾ cup water to a boil in a saucepan. Reduce the heat to low, cover, and boil gently for 5 minutes. Transfer the sauce to a bowl, and emulsify it with a hand blender. Add the ¼ teaspoon each salt and pepper, the ½ teaspoon sugar, and the butter, blending the mixture until it is smooth. This will yield 2¼ cups.

12 Let the fish rest on the pan for 10 minutes before slicing and serving it. Serve one thick slice per person, adding some of the sauce.

Note: If the dough cracks while baking or when cutting the fish into slices, sponge up any juices that seep out of the fish with paper towels.

Raspberry Cookie Dough *Galette*

This *galette* is made with *pâte sucrée,* or cookie dough, which produces a delicate and buttery crust that keeps well enough so that it can withstand 4 to 5 hours on a buffet table before softening. Conventionally, the dough is cooked ahead of time, and then raw berries or poached fruit is arranged on top not long before it is served. The crust is sometimes lined with a pastry cream before the fruit is added, and often (as here) the fruit is finished with a glaze. For this recipe, the "less perfect" berries are combined with raspberry preserves and spread over the cooked shell before the nicest berries are arranged on top.

PÂTE SUCRÉE

- 1¾ **cups all-purpose flour (10 to 10½ ounces)**
- 1⅓ **sticks unsalted butter (5⅓ ounces), softened**
- 3 **tablespoons confectioners' sugar**
- 1 **egg yolk**
- 1 **to 2 tablespoons water**

FILLING AND GLAZE

- 4 **cups fresh raspberries**
- 1 **cup seedless raspberry preserves**
- 1 **tablespoon raspberry brandy**

1 Preheat the oven to 375 degrees.

2 *For the dough:* Combine the flour, butter, and sugar together in a bowl, mixing the ingredients with a spoon or breaking them into pieces with your hands until they are mixed together coarsely. In a small bowl, mix together the egg yolk and water, and add to the flour mixture.

3 Gather the ingredients together and, using the technique known as *fraisage,* with the heel of your hand smear about 3 tablespoons of the dough forward at a time on a board or countertop until all the ingredients are blended and the dough is completely smooth and the same color throughout. Repeat this *fraisage* procedure a

(continued)

TOTAL TIME
2 hours, including cooking time

YIELD
6 to 8 servings

NUTRITIONAL ANALYSIS PER SERVING

Calories 505.2
Protein 5.3 gm.
Carbohydrates 68.7 gm.
Fat 24.5 gm.
Saturated fat 14.6 gm.
Cholesterol 92.5 mg.
Sodium 254.2 mg.

"Baking is something that I don't do very much of. But I remember baking Toll-House cookies one time and my father came in, tasted them, and said, 'No, it's wrong.' I said, 'No, they're Toll-House cookies—I'm following the recipe, and I've measured everything painstakingly.' I made my Toll-House cookies and they tasted exactly the way they they were supposed to taste!"

second time to make sure the ingredients are well combined.

4   Place the dough in the center of a piece of plastic wrap about 14 inches square, and place another piece of plastic wrap the same size on top. Roll the dough between the two pieces of plastic wrap until it forms a circle about 14 inches in diameter. Peel off the top sheet of plastic wrap, and invert the dough onto a cookie sheet. Pull off the remaining sheet of plastic wrap.

5   Roll the edge of the dough inward on itself to create a border about ½ inch thick all around. Press on the border so that it is tapered at the top, and, using your thumb and index finger, pinch all around the edge to create a decorative border.

6   Place the dough in the 375-degree oven, and bake it for about 30 minutes, until it is nicely browned and cooked through. (The recipe can be completed to this point up to 12 hours ahead.)

7   *For the filling:* Using any damaged or soft berries, mix about 1½ cups

of the berries with 4 tablespoons of the preserves in a bowl. Not more than 2 hours ahead of serving, spread the mixture over the base of the cooked tart shell. Arrange the remaining berries on top so that they cover the entire surface of the tart.

8   *For the glaze:* Mix together in a small bowl the remaining preserves (about ¾ cup) and the brandy. Using a spoon and brush, coat the top of the berries with the mixture.

9   Cut the *galette* into wedges with a sharp knife (it has a tendency to break when cut), before serving.

The Seafood Lesson

Poached Swordfish with Lemon-Parsley Sauce

Mushroom-Stuffed Squid

Breaded and Broiled Red Snapper

Mangoes with Cognac

Jacques 96

Because Claudine doesn't feel comfortable about cooking fish or shellfish, she requested a demonstration. I designed this lesson, consisting of three fish dishes, to illustrate and clarify some aspects of fish cookery. This is not a menu per se, although we do conclude with a dessert.

Use the freshest fish and the best quality olive oil, preferably extra-virgin, for the poached swordfish. Although the sauce can be made up a few hours ahead, in that case reserve the parsley—it tends to discolor if added too soon because of the acidity of the lemon juice. Be sure to drain off any liquid that has accumulated around the fish before spooning on the sauce; this will prevent its flavor from becoming diluted.

The second dish features squid stuffed with mushrooms and coated with a sauce before cooking. Available year-round fresh or frozen, squid are relatively inexpensive. Even though they already come from the market cleaned, it is important to wash the squid well before stuffing them.

The mushroom stuffing is relatively simple to prepare. When opened and somewhat black underneath, large regular mushrooms have great flavor that is delicious in dishes like this. I sauté them with onions, garlic, thyme, and the reserved wings of the squid. The mixture is then seasoned, and coarsely chopped leftover bread is tossed in lightly just at the end.

CLAUDINE:

～

"I think I'll cook fish at home now that I've had this lesson. I love fish: I have cooked it, but when I try to do something a little more adventurous, I usually end up with a mess. Putting it en croûte *with potatoes, now, that's easy—that I can do."*

The tomato-based sauce for the squid is seasoned with fresh oregano and a sprinkling of saffron pistils—preferably pistils from Spain, which I think are the best. Saffron is an expensive spice, but its wonderful flavor makes it worth the investment.

Red snapper fillets are breaded and broiled in our next demonstration dish. Delicate and mild, snapper is available almost year-round; it's best purchased from a good fishmonger.

For dessert, I suggest slivers of mango lightly sweetened and tossed with a little lime juice, lime peel, and Cognac. Especially good after chilling, this light, refreshing dish is the perfect finish to our lesson on seafood.

WINES

WHITE

Kendall Jackson,
Grand Reserve, Viognier

Joseph Drouhin, Domaine de Vaudon,
Chablis

Poached Swordfish with Lemon-Parsley Sauce

Poached swordfish is served here in a refreshing lemon-parsley sauce. I like swordfish, particularly if it is not overcooked (which tends to make it dry). Served as a first course, 4 to 5 ounces of fish per person is sufficient. If you want to serve the swordfish as a main course, double the ingredients.

LEMON-PARSLEY SAUCE

- 1½ tablespoons lemon juice (juice of 1 large or 2 small lemons)
- 2 tablespoons extra-virgin olive oil
- 1½ tablespoons hot water
- ⅓ teaspoon salt
- ¼ teaspoon freshly ground black pepper
- ¼ cup chopped fresh flat-leaf parsley

- 4 pieces swordfish, each about 4 to 5 ounces and 1¼ inches thick (16 to 20 ounces total)

1 Mix the lemon-parsley sauce ingredients together thoroughly in a small bowl, and set the sauce aside for up to 30 minutes. (If preparing the sauce further ahead, wait to add the parsley until just before serving; otherwise the lemon juice in the mixture will tend to yellow it.)

2 At serving time, bring 6 cups of water to a boil in a large saucepan. Holding the fish fillets with a slotted spoon or skimmer, lower them individually into the pan, and bring the water back to a boil. Reduce the heat to very low, and poach the fish, cooking the pieces at a very light boil for 3 to 4 minutes, until they are barely cooked through.

3 Using a slotted spoon or skimmer, lift the fish from the water, drain thoroughly, and arrange one fillet on each of four warm plates.

4 Spoon the sauce over the fish, dividing it equally among the servings. Serve immediately.

TOTAL TIME
10 minutes

YIELD
4 first-course servings

NUTRITIONAL ANALYSIS PER SERVING

Calories 234.6
Protein 28.2 gm.
Carbohydrates 0.8 gm.
Fat 12.7 gm.
Saturated fat 2.6 gm.
Cholesterol 55.3 mg.
Sodium 310.4 mg.

Mushroom-Stuffed Squid

Most squid from the supermarket is already cleaned. If yours are not, follow the instructions for cleaning them in the recipe.

Whether you fill the squid with the stuffing using a spoon or a pastry bag, it is important that you not overstuff them. Two to three tablespoons of filling is sufficient; the body will look about half full initially, but since the body shrinks as it cooks, and the stuffing expands, the squid will be properly stuffed when ready to serve. After the opening on each is secured with a toothpick, the squid are arranged in one layer in a large, deep skillet and cooked gently in the sauce.

TOTAL TIME
2 hours (including cooling time)

YIELD
4 servings

NUTRITIONAL ANALYSIS PER SERVING
Calories 267.5
Protein 25.9 gm.
Carbohydrates 23.5 gm.
Fat 8.0 gm.
Saturated fat 1.3 gm.
Cholesterol 330.6 mg.
Sodium 485.7 mg.

1¼ **pounds medium squid, 5 to 6 inches long (about 8)**

1½ **tablespoons virgin olive oil**

1 **medium onion (6 ounces), peeled and coarsely chopped (1¼ cups)**

1 **stalk celery, washed and coarsely chopped (¼ cup)**

6 **ounces mushrooms, washed and coarsely chopped (2 cups)**

2 **large cloves garlic, peeled and thinly sliced (1 tablespoon)**

1½ **teaspoons chopped fresh thyme, or ½ teaspoon dried thyme**

½ **teaspoon salt**

½ **teaspoon freshly ground black pepper**

1½ **ounces leftover bread (2 slices), coarsely chopped (¾ cup)**

2 **tomatoes (about 1 pound), cut into large chunks**

2 **tablespoons tomato paste**

1½ **teaspoons chopped fresh oregano, or ½ teaspoon dried oregano**

1 **teaspoon saffron pistils, crumbled**

1 If the squid are not cleaned, separate the tentacles from the bodies. Remove the black skin from the bodies by rubbing it off under cold water. Clean the inside of each body or sac by rinsing it under cold water. Remove the beak from the hole in the center of each tentacle, and separate the "wings" or flaps from the body or sac. (You should have approximately 10 ounces of bodies, 6 ounces of tentacles, and 2 ounces of wings.) Chop the wings coarsely (you will have about ¼ cup), and reserve for the stuffing.

2 Heat the oil in a saucepan. When it is hot, add the onion and celery. Cook for 2 minutes, then add the mushrooms, garlic, thyme, and wings. Reduce the heat to low, cover, and cook for 8 minutes.

3 Remove the lid, add half the salt and pepper, and cook for another 2 to 3 minutes, if needed, for most of the moisture to evaporate. Stir in the bread gently, and cool to lukewarm.

4 When the stuffing mixture is cool enough to handle, stuff it loosely into the squid bodies, taking care to fill them only partially, since during cooking the stuffing will expand and the squid will shrink slightly. Secure the open ends of the squid with wooden toothpicks, and arrange them in one layer in a large skillet or saucepan. Arrange the tentacles around the squid.

5 Place the tomato chunks in the bowl of food processor with the tomato paste and the remaining salt and pepper. Process for a few seconds to create a sauce.

6 Pour the sauce over the squid, and sprinkle on the oregano and saffron. Bring the mixture to a boil over high heat, then reduce the heat to low, cover, and cook for 15 to 20 minutes at a very gentle boil.

7 Serve immediately. This goes well with couscous, rice, potatoes, or noodles.

CLAUDINE:

~

"Watching my father, I'm always very excited to find out that, yes, I can also make whatever it is that he's making. He brings gourmet cooking down to earth in a manner so that anybody can do it."

Breaded and Broiled Red Snapper

It's important to make fresh bread crumbs for this recipe using bread that is one or two days old yet still somewhat moist. Do not use commercially packaged dry bread crumbs—they do not contain any moisture and are much more concentrated than fresh bread crumbs. A slice of regular white bread processed in a food processor will yield about ½ to ⅔ cup of crumbs, but if that same slice of bread is first cut into cubes and dried in the oven before it is processed, it will produce only 2 to 3 tablespoons of crumbs. Thus, you would need 3 times more dry bread crumbs than fresh to bread the fish for this recipe

TOTAL TIME

15 minutes

YIELD

4 servings

NUTRITIONAL ANALYSIS PER SERVING

Calories 342.1
Protein 37.8 gm.
Carbohydrates 18.2 gm.
Fat 13.0 gm.
Saturated fat 3.4 gm.
Cholesterol 71.0 mg.
Sodium 676.1 mg.

2   **cloves garlic, peeled**

4   **slices white bread (4 ounces), 1 or 2 days old, broken into pieces**

4   **or 5 scallions, cleaned, trimmed (most of the green left on), and minced fine (⅓ cup)**

½   **teaspoon freshly ground black pepper**

¾   **teaspoon salt**

2   **tablespoons virgin olive oil**

1   **tablespoon unsalted butter, melted**

4   **red snapper fillets, each about 6 ounces and ¾ inch thick**

1   **lemon, cut into 4 wedges**

1   Preheat the broiler.

2   Place the garlic cloves in the bowl of a food processor, and process until fine. Add the bread slices, and process them into crumbs. (You should have 2½ cups.) Transfer the garlic and bread crumbs to a bowl, and mix in the scallions, pepper, and salt. Add the oil and butter, and rub the mixture gently between your hands to moisten the bread crumbs. The mixture should be loose.

3   Arrange the fillets side by side on a nonstick baking sheet. Cover them with half the crumbs, patting the crumbs lightly over the surface of the fillets. Place the fillets under the preheated broiler about 5 inches from the heat, and

cook them for 2 to 3 minutes, until the crumbs are nicely browned.

4 Gently turn the pieces of fish over with a spatula, and pat the remaining seasoned bread crumbs lightly over their surface. Then place the fillets under the broiler for another 2 to 3 minutes. The crumbs should be thoroughly browned and the fish just cooked through. Since cooking time will vary depending on the thickness of the fillets, check to see if they are done by cutting into one. If more cooking is needed, turn off the broiler, and let the fish remain in the hot oven for 3 to 4 minutes.

5 Serve immediately, one fillet per person, with a wedge of lemon.

Mangoes with Cognac

This simple but elegant mango dessert is a sure winner, provided it is made with a ripe mango. Mangoes are available year-round now, but are usually of better quality at summer's end.

If you have any dessert left over, puree it in a food processor, and spread it on toast for breakfast the following morning.

TOTAL TIME
10 minutes, plus 2 hours chilling time (optional)

YIELD
4 servings

NUTRITIONAL ANALYSIS PER SERVING
Calories 134.3
Protein 0.6 gm.
Carbohydrates 30.3 gm.
Fat 0.3 gm.
Saturated fat 0.1 gm.
Cholesterol 0 mg.
Sodium 4.4 mg.

2 **ripe mangoes (about 12 ounces each)**

2 **to 3 strips lime peel (green part only), removed with a vegetable peeler or zester**

3 **tablespoons sugar**

2 **tablespoons Cognac, rum, or whiskey**

3 **tablespoons lime juice**

1 Peel the mangoes, cutting deeply enough into the fruit so that any green-colored flesh is also removed. Then, cutting inward, toward the pit, slice each of the mangoes into slivers about ½ inch thick. Discard the pits.

2 Julienne the lime peel strips: Stack them up together, and cut them into thin "sticks." (You should have about 1 tablespoon of julienned peel.)

3 In a bowl, combine the mango slivers with the sugar, Cognac, and lime juice.

4 Either serve immediately or, for added flavor, chill for at least 2 hours, stirring occasionally, before serving. Serve in chilled glasses, sprinkled with the julienned peel.

Cooking Like a Pro

Fusilli with Escarole,
Eggplant, and Olive Sauce

Sole and Scallop Ensemble

Potato Slabs with "Tapenade"

Warm chocolate fondue
Soufflé

Jacques 96

This ensemble of dishes is not necessarily a menu, but rather my way of showing Claudine the preparation of dishes she likes but is hesitant to serve because she is not familiar with how they are made. As a result, several of the recipes are extremely versatile.

Included here are two dishes of the type you might order when out at a restaurant. The sole and scallop ensemble makes a beautiful main course for a special dinner party. Ideal for dessert at the same meal would be the warm chocolate soufflé, which can be made ahead, reheats well, and is easy to serve.

The pasta dish, served here as a first course, can stand on its own and be served as a main dish. Conversely, the potato slabs, presented here as a side dish, would make a nice first course. Kalamata olives appear in both the pasta and potato dishes, so you may want to serve only one of these dishes as part of a menu.

WINES

WHITE
Joseph Drouhin,
Pouilly-Fuissé

SPARKLING
Kristone, Blanc de Blancs

Fusilli with Escarole, Eggplant, and Olive Sauce

Pasta is one of the most versatile ingredients available to the cook. I combine it here with a sauce made of olives, escarole, eggplant, pignoli nuts, garlic, and peas because that was what was available the day I created it. On another day, depending on the contents of my refrigerator, red onion, zucchini, green pepper, tomato, and broccoli could find their way into this recipe along with capers or anchovy fillets. Feel free to experiment with the sauce ingredients for this dish, and try some of the different pasta shapes the market offers as well.

TOTAL TIME
60 to 80 minutes

YIELD
4 servings

NUTRITIONAL ANALYSIS PER SERVING

Calories 649.8
Protein 15.8 gm.
Carbohydrates 82.3 gm.
Fat 29.9 gm.
Saturated fat 3.9 gm.
Cholesterol 0 mg.
Sodium 1,007.6 mg.

ESCAROLE, EGGPLANT, AND OLIVE SAUCE

- 1 eggplant (about 1 pound)
- ½ teaspoon salt
- 1 tablespoon canola oil
- 4 tablespoons extra-virgin olive oil
- 2½ tablespoons pignoli nuts
- 3 cloves garlic, peeled and thinly sliced (2 tablespoons)
- 10 ounces escarole (about ½ an escarole), cut into 2-inch pieces (about 6 cups, loose), washed and drained
- ½ cup tiny peas (fresh or frozen)
- 24 whole kalamata olives, pitted
- ¼ teaspoon freshly ground black pepper
- 12 cups water (for cooking the pasta)
- 12 ounces dry fusilli (3 cups)
- ½ teaspoon salt
- ½ teaspoon freshly ground black pepper

Grated Parmesan cheese

1. Preheat the oven to 400 degrees.

2. Trim off and discard the ends of the eggplant, and cut it lengthwise into 5 slices of about equal thickness. Sprinkle the slices with ¼ teaspoon of the salt. Line a baking sheet with aluminum foil, and coat the foil with the canola oil.

3. Press the slices of eggplant into the oil on the baking sheet, then turn them over (so they are lightly oiled on both sides), and arrange them in a single layer on the sheet. Place the eggplant in the 400-degree oven for 40 minutes, until the slices are very tender and slightly browned. When they are cool enough to handle, remove the slices from the sheet, and cut them into 1½-inch pieces (about 1½ cups).

4. Heat the olive oil in a large skillet. Add the pignoli nuts and the garlic, and sauté for about 20 seconds. Add the escarole, still wet from the washing, cover, and cook over medium to high heat for 3 to 4 minutes, until the escarole is wilted and starting to brown. Add the peas, olives, eggplant, the remaining ¼ teaspoon salt, and the ¼ teaspoon pepper. Mix well, and set aside. (This can be done up to 1 hour ahead.)

5. At serving time, bring the water to a boil in a pot. Add the pasta, and bring the water back to a boil over high heat. Cook, uncovered, for 10 to 12 minutes, until tender. Remove ½ cup of the cooking liquid from the pasta, and add it to the sauce mixture. Drain the pasta.

6. Combine the pasta with the sauce and the ½ teaspoon each salt and pepper. Mix well. Divide among four plates, sprinkle with the grated Parmesan, and serve immediately.

CLAUDINE:

~

"My father's philosophy on food: good, fresh, natural, and don't torture the food. If you can close your eyes and know what you're eating, then it's probably good. It's supposed to taste like what it is. It's not supposed to be mangled and pureed and tortured into something else."

Sole and Scallop Ensemble

The time of cooking will depend on the thickness of the fillets. If preparing the dish ahead, slightly undercook the sole so it can wait (up to 1 hour), covered, in a warm oven before serving.

TOTAL TIME
1 hour

YIELD
4 servings

**NUTRITIONAL
ANALYSIS
PER SERVING**

Calories 341.4
Protein 39.4 gm.
Carbohydrates 9.1 gm.
Fat 14.6 gm.
Saturated fat 6.3 gm.
Cholesterol 116.6 mg.
Sodium 478.7 mg.

4 **fillets of grey or lemon sole, or flounder (1 pound)**

4 **large scallops (about 5 ounces), washed**

LEEK AND MUSHROOM STUFFING

1 **small leek (about 4 ounces), trimmed (with most of the green left on), thinly sliced, and washed (1¼ cups)**

2 **ounces mushrooms, washed and thinly sliced (1 cup)**

1 **tablespoon virgin olive oil**

¼ **teaspoon salt**

3 **tablespoons chopped shallots**

8 **ounces cherry tomatoes, quartered**

¼ **teaspoon salt**

⅓ **cup dry, fruity white wine**

3 **tablespoons unsalted butter**

1 **tablespoon chopped fresh chives**

1 Preheat the oven to 425 degrees.

2 Divide each fillet in half by removing and discarding the small connecting strip of cartilage down the center. Pound the fillets to a thickness of about ¼ inch throughout. Pair up the fillets by size, matching smaller with smaller, and larger with larger. Cut each scallop into 4 horizontal slices, and set the slices aside.

3 *For the leek and mushroom stuffing:* Place the leek, still wet from washing, in a skillet with the mushrooms, oil, and the ¼ teaspoon salt. Cook, covered, over medium heat for 5 to 6 minutes, until the moisture is gone from the pan and the mixture is starting to sizzle. Set aside to cool.

4 Arrange 4 single fillets on the work surface, white side down, and spread the stuffing mixture on top, dividing it evenly among the fillets. Cover the stuffing

with the slices of scallop, then arrange the remaining fillets (the mates to those on the work surface) on top, white side up, to make 4 "sandwiches."

5 Sprinkle the shallots and tomatoes evenly in a large ovenproof skillet, and arrange the fillet sandwiches on top in one layer. Sprinkle with the ¼ teaspoon salt, and add the wine.

6 Cut a piece of parchment paper the size of the skillet, and lay it on top of the fillets.

7 Bring the fish to a strong boil on top of the stove, then place them in the 425-degree oven for 6 to 7 minutes, until they are just cooked through. Reduce the oven temperature to 170 degrees, or preheat a second oven to 170 degrees. Using a large, flat spatula, transfer the fillets to an ovenproof platter (reserving the cooking juices), and place them in the 170-degree oven to keep them warm while you complete the recipe.

8 Bring the reserved cooking juices to a boil in the skillet. (You should have 1¼ to 1½ cups; if you have

more than this, boil the mixture until it is reduced to this amount.) Transfer the stock and solids to a bowl or large measuring cup, and emulsify them with a hand blender until smooth. Strain, add the butter, and emulsify again with the blender until smooth.

9 Arrange a portion of fish on each of four individual plates, and discard any juices that have collected around the fish on the platter. Coat the fish with the sauce, sprinkle the chives on top, and serve immediately.

Potato Slabs with *Tapenade*

No salt is added to the potatoes in this recipe because the topping is salty enough to season the potatoes as well. The potato slabs can be served without the *tapenade* as an accompaniment to meat or poultry. If serving the potatoes on their own, however, add ½ teaspoon of salt to the cooking liquid at the beginning of the recipe.

TOTAL TIME
30 minutes

YIELD
4 servings

NUTRITIONAL ANALYSIS PER SERVING

Calories 317.4
Protein 7.3 gm.
Carbohydrates 42.1 gm.
Fat 13.8 gm.
Saturated fat 3.3 gm.
Cholesterol 11.7 mg.
Sodium 892.4 mg.

4   **baking potatoes, about 8 ounces each**
1   **tablespoon virgin olive oil**
1   **tablespoon unsalted butter**
¾   **cup water**

TAPENADE
⅔   **cup whole kalamata olives, pitted (about 20)**
2   **cloves garlic, peeled**
3   **tablespoons drained capers**
½   **(2-ounce) can anchovy fillets in oil**
2   **scallions, cleaned and finely minced (¼ cup)**
¼   **teaspoon freshly ground black pepper**

1   **tablespoon minced fresh chives**

1   Trim each potato lengthwise on two opposite long sides, then cut each potato in half lengthwise to create two slabs, each about 1 inch thick. Arrange the potatoes, with the larger cut side of each down, in one layer in a very large nonstick skillet.

2   Add the oil, butter, and water to the skillet, and bring the mixture to a boil over high heat. Cover, reduce the heat to medium, and cook for 15 minutes. All of the water should be gone at this point; keep cooking the potato slabs, uncovered, for 1 or 2 minutes longer, until they are well browned on the underside. Turn the potato slabs over, and cook them over low heat, covered, for about 10 to 12 minutes longer to brown them on the other side.

3 Meanwhile, place all the *tapenade* ingredients in the bowl of a food processor, and pulse the switch for about 20 seconds, until the mixture is well combined but still chunky. This will yield about 1 cup.

4 When the potato slabs are tender, moist, and nicely browned on both sides, transfer them to a large serving plate, and spoon about 1 tablespoon of the *tapenade* mixture on top of each. Sprinkle with the chives, and serve immediately, two slabs per person.

Warm Chocolate Fondue Soufflé

Both its texture and taste give this recipe elements of soufflé, cake, and pudding. The chocolate mixture should be slightly runny in the center when the dessert is served.

TOTAL TIME
30 minutes, plus
resting time

YIELD.
4 servings

NUTRITIONAL ANALYSIS PER SERVING
Calories 235.4
Protein 4.7 gm.
Carbohydrates 16.8 gm.
Fat 18.5 gm.
Saturated fat 10.1 gm.
Cholesterol 129.5 mg.
Sodium 32.7 mg.

3 **ounces bittersweet chocolate**

3 **tablespoons unsalted butter, with ½ teaspoon reserved**

1½ **tablespoons sugar**

2 **eggs, separated**

1 **teaspoon vanilla**

4 **tablespoons sour cream (optional)**

1 Preheat the oven to 350 degrees.

2 Heat about 2 cups of water in a small saucepan. Place the chocolate, butter (minus the ½ teaspoon), and 1 tablespoon of the sugar in an ovenproof bowl, and place the bowl over the hot water in the pan until they are melted. (Alternatively, melt the chocolate, butter, and sugar in a preheated 180-degree oven or in a microwave oven.)

3 Beat the egg whites until they hold a soft peak, then add the remaining ½ tablespoon of sugar and beat for another 5 seconds. (The whites should not be too stiff.) Add the yolks and the vanilla to the melted chocolate mixture, and mix them in well. Then add the beaten whites, and stir and mix them in with a rubber spatula until well combined.

4 Place 4 small ovenproof bowls (1 cup capacity) or aluminum cupcake molds on a cookie sheet and butter the molds with the reserved ½ teaspoon of butter. Divide the batter among the cups, and bake them in the 350-degree oven for 10 to 12 minutes (the soufflés still should be soft in the center). Let them rest for about 10 minutes, then unmold them onto four individual dessert plates.

5 Serve each dessert with 1 tablespoon of sour cream on top, if desired.

Note: To make the desserts up to 24 hours ahead, bake for 8 to 10 minutes only, then cool, cover, and refrigerate. When ready to serve, heat the unmolded desserts in a preheated 350-degree oven for 5 minutes or until warm inside.

The Duck Party

Duck and Beans Casserole

Duck Liver Pâté

Mock Peking Duck

Sautéed Duck in Vinegar Sauce

Rhubarb and Strawberry Coulis

Jacques 96

This lesson, which is not a menu per se, is intended to demonstrate how to understand ingredients and the process of cooking, and how to cook economically with delicious results. The duck exemplifies how ingredients can be used to their fullest. It is transformed into four dishes, three of which can be served as main courses.

After the duck is skinned and boned, each part finds its way into a separate, original recipe that serves from four to six people. The meat is sautéed and served with a vinegar-flavored sauce, the skin is turned into my version of Peking duck, the bones and neck become part of a bean casserole, and the liver is transformed into a pâté.

WINES

WHITE

Camelot, Chardonnay

RED

Cambria, Tepusquet Vineyard, Sangiovese

The important point here is that a good cook could create four totally *different* recipes from the same basic ingredient. For example, the duck skin could be transformed into crackling for use as a garnish on soup or salad; the bones could be used to create a stock, sauce, or soup; the liver could be cooked briefly and served on toast; and the meat could be sautéed and served with a Cognac, green pepper, or olive sauce.

Practicing such economy in the kitchen is absolutely essential for the professional chef as well as the good home cook.

Rhubarb and strawberry, always a wonderful combination, are particularly delicious when cooked together, as they are here, and served as a fruit soup, or *coulis*.

Starting the Menu: The Whole Duck

1 duck, about 5½ pounds, with the liver, gizzard, neck, and heart

BASIC PREPARATIONS

1 Remove the liver, gizzard, neck, and heart (about 1 pound total) from the duck, and set them aside.

DIVIDING THE DUCK

2 Remove both wings of the duck at the shoulder joints, and set the wings aside with the gizzard, neck, and heart.

3 Cut a slit the length of the duck along the backbone, and, using a sharp paring knife, separate the skin from the meat and carcass. (Do not worry if you make a few holes in the skin, but try to remove it in 1 or 2 pieces.) Set the skin aside.

4 Remove the two legs at the hip joint, and pull off the breast meat. Remove the bones, and pull out as many sinews from the legs as you can. (You will have approximately 1¼ pounds of skinless, boneless meat from the 2 boned legs and the breasts.) Wrap the meat well in plastic wrap, and refrigerate it until cooking time. Set the carcass aside with the gizzard, neck, heart, and wings.

5 Place the liver (about 3 ounces) and an equal amount of fat (the two lumps of fat from the rear opening will weigh about 3 ounces) in a small bowl. Cover and set aside.

6 The duck is now divided into four separate groupings: meat; skin; liver and fat; and carcass, gizzard, neck, heart, and wings. Each grouping will be used to create a different recipe.

CLAUDINE:

~

"We've always eaten a lot of duck at home, and I love it roasted as well as in a stew. It's really easy to turn into impressive dishes, and it's wonderful."

Sautéed Duck in Vinegar Sauce

This is a classic dish, complex and flavorful. Nonetheless, it takes only a few minutes to prepare—provided you have the right ingredients and know the proper cooking techniques.

2   tablespoons unsalted butter

2   skinless, boneless duck legs
    (from duck, opposite)

2   skinless, boneless duck breasts
    (from duck, opposite)

¼   teaspoon salt

¼   teaspoon freshly ground black
    pepper

2   tablespoons chopped onion

1   teaspoon chopped garlic
    (2 cloves)

⅓   cup dry red wine

3   tablespoons balsamic vinegar

2   tablespoons ketchup

1   tablespoon A-1 steak sauce

¼   cup water

1   tablespoon minced fresh chives

1   Heat the butter in a large skillet, and sprinkle the duck with the salt and pepper. When the butter is hot, add the duck leg meat to the skillet, and cook it for 3½ minutes on each side. After 2 minutes, add the breast meat, cook for 2½ minutes, turn, and cook for 2½ minutes on the other side.

2   Transfer the duck to an ovenproof plate, and place it in a 180-degree oven to rest and keep warm while you make the sauce.

3   Add the onion and garlic to the drippings in the skillet, and cook, stirring constantly, for 15 to 20 seconds. Add the wine and vinegar, and cook until the liquid is reduced to about ¼ cup.

4   Add the ketchup, steak sauce, and water, bring to a boil, and cook for 1 minute. Drain off any liquid that has accumulated around the meat, and add it to the sauce.

5   Arrange the meat from half a leg and half a breast on each of four plates, and coat with the sauce. Sprinkle with the chives, and serve immediately.

TOTAL TIME
10 to 12 minutes

YIELD
4 servings

**NUTRITIONAL
ANALYSIS
PER SERVING**

Calories 268.7
Protein 26.3 gm.
Carbohydrates 4.3 gm.
Fat 14.2 gm.
Saturated fat 6.9 gm.
Cholesterol 124.8 mg.
Sodium 394.2 mg.

Mock Peking Duck

Although most restaurants serve the whole duck as part of Peking duck, wrapping pieces of the meat in Chinese pancakes, my version uses only the skin of the duck, which I present in pancakes as well. My wife and I ate a version similar to this in Beijing several years ago.

TOTAL TIME
About 1½ hours

YIELD
6 servings
(2 pancakes apiece)

NUTRITIONAL ANALYSIS PER SERVING
Calories 189.1
Protein 3.7 gm.
Carbohydrates 33.8 gm.
Fat 3.4 gm.
Saturated fat 0.5 gm.
Cholesterol 0 mg.
Sodium 282.0 mg.

Skin from the duck (see page 98)

¼ teaspoon salt

½ teaspoon sugar dissolved in 1 tablespoon water

PANCAKES

1½ cups all-purpose flour

½ to ⅔ cup boiling water

1 teaspoon dark sesame oil

HOISIN-SESAME SAUCE

⅓ cup hoisin sauce

1 tablespoon sesame oil

2 tablespoons water

GARNISHES

4 scallions, cleaned, and each cut lengthwise into three pieces

1 small cucumber (about 10 ounces), peeled, split lengthwise, seeded, and cut lengthwise into 12 strips

⅓ cup cilantro leaves

1 Preheat the oven to 375 degrees.

2 Bring 4 quarts of water to a boil. Lower the duck skin into the boiling water (the water will stop boiling). Cook the skin over high heat in the hot water, turning it occasionally with tongs, for 2 to 3 minutes, until the water is just beginning to boil again.

3 Lift the skin from the water, and spread it out, flesh side down, as flat as possible, on a jelly roll pan. Sprinkle it with the salt, and moisten it with the sweetened water. Place in the 375-degree oven for 45 to 55 minutes, until the skin is crispy and brown.

4 Remove the skin from the pan, reserving the fat (I had 1 cup of clear fat), if desired. (The fat is good for sautéing potatoes, browning meat prior to roasting, or for covering the Duck Liver Pâté [page 104], if you plan to

keep the pâté for more than 3 or 4 days.)

5   When the skin is cool enough to handle, cut it into 12 long strips, arrange it on an ovenproof platter, and place it in a warm oven until serving time.

6   *For the pancakes:* Place the flour in the bowl of a food processor, and add the boiling water. Process for 15 to 20 seconds, until the mixture forms into a ball. (Depending on the amount of moisture in the flour, you may need a little more or a little less water.)

7   Remove the dough from the food processor, knead it for a few seconds, and form it into a cylinder 6 inches long by 2 inches wide. Cut the cylinder crosswise into 12 slices, each about ⅜ inch thick. Brush 6 of the rounds with some of the dark sesame oil, and arrange the remaining 6 rounds on top of the oiled rounds. Press each of these pancake "sandwiches" together, and extend them to create 6 pancakes, each 3 to 4 inches in diameter. Using the remainder of the dark sesame oil, lightly oil a small area

of your countertop, and roll each pancake on this oiled area to extend it into a 7-inch disk.

8   Heat a large, sturdy skillet until hot, and cook the pancake sandwiches one at a time in the skillet for 45 seconds to 1 minute per side, until lightly browned.

9   When the pancake sandwiches are cooked, pull them apart so you have 12 individual pancakes again. (The oil in the middle of the dough rounds makes them separate easily.) Fold each pancake, crusty side in, into quarters. Arrange the pancakes in one slightly overlapping layer on a plate, cover with plastic wrap, and set aside.

10 In a small bowl, combine the ingredients for the hoisin-sesame sauce.

11 Just before serving time, remove the plastic wrap, and set the plate containing the pancakes in a steamer set over a pan of boiling water. Steam, covered, for 3 to 4 minutes, until the pancakes are hot. Alternatively, moisten the pancakes with about 1 tablespoon of water, cover, and heat in a microwave oven for 30 seconds

(continued)

(warming the pancakes in a microwave tends to make them chewier than steaming them).

12 To serve, unfold the pancakes, place a piece of duck skin, a scallion strip, a cucumber strip, a scant tablespoon each of hoisin-sesame sauce and cilantro leaves in the center of each, and roll into a cylinder. Repeat this procedure with the remaining pancakes. Serve immediately.

Duck and Beans Casserole

This recipe is essentially a "poor man's cassoulet," a version of the famous dish from the southwest of France that is traditionally made with beans, sausages, preserved goose, duck, pork, and lamb. Yet, this quick version is satisfying, economical, and close enough in taste to the classic rendition to make it well worth preparing.

8 ounces navy or Great Northern dried beans

Carcass, gizzard, neck, heart, and wings from the duck (see page 98)

1¼ teaspoons salt

1 bay leaf

½ teaspoon *herbes de Provence*

4 cups cold water

1 medium leek (6 to 7 ounces), split, washed, trimmed, and cut into 1-inch pieces (2 cups)

1 medium onion (6 ounces), peeled and cut into ½-inch pieces (1 cup)

2 carrots (6 ounces), peeled and cut into ½-inch pieces (¾ cup)

¼ teaspoon Tabasco hot pepper sauce

3 to 4 large cloves garlic, peeled, crushed, and chopped (1 tablespoon)

¼ cup chopped fresh parsley

1½ cups diced (1-inch) tomatoes

1 Rinse the beans in cool water, and place them in a pot with the carcass, gizzard, neck, heart, and wings of the duck. Add the salt, bay leaf, *herbes de Provence,* and water. Bring to a boil, cover, reduce the heat to very low, and cook at a gentle boil for 1 hour. (The beans should be almost cooked, but still a bit crunchy.)

2 Remove the carcass, neck, gizzard, heart, and wings from the pot, and let them cool on a platter to lukewarm. Meanwhile, add the leek, onion, and carrots to the pot, and bring the mixture back to a boil. Cover, reduce the heat to low, and boil gently for 20 minutes.

3 Meanwhile, pick any meat from the cooled carcass bones and wings, and cut it coarsely along with the gizzard and heart (you should have 1½ to 2 cups of meat). Add it all back to the beans while they are cooking with the vegetables.

4 After this mixture has cooked for 20 minutes, add the Tabasco sauce. Combine the garlic and parsley in a small bowl, then add the mixture to the pot along with the tomatoes.

5 The beans should be soft and tender at this point, and the mixture should be soupy but not overly liquid in consistency. If it is too watery, boil it gently, uncovered, for 10 to 15 minutes. (If you are making this dish ahead for later serving, remember that it will have a tendency to thicken when reheated.) If the dish is too thick, thin it a little by adding a few tablespoons of water.

6 Serve immediately on soup plates.

Variation: For a more authentic cassoulet, divide the mixture, which should be very soupy, among 6 small earthenware tureens (like those you would use for onion soup), place a 1-inch slice of kielbasa sausage and 1 link of pork sausage in each bowl. Top each with 1 teaspoon of dried bread crumbs, arrange the bowls on a tray, and place in a preheated 350-degree oven for about 45 minutes.

TOTAL TIME
1 hour 45 minutes

YIELD
8 cups (enough for 6 main-course servings)

NUTRITIONAL ANALYSIS PER SERVING
Calories 326.2
Protein 19.4 gm.
Carbohydrates 32.7 gm.
Fat 13.4 gm.
Saturated fat 4.5 gm.
Cholesterol 51.8 mg.
Sodium 506.9 mg.

Duck Liver Pâté

This may not be as good as a true *foie gras,* but it's similar enough in flavor for a dish that costs only pennies to make. Not only can the pâté be served on toast—it can also serve as a finish for a classic Beef Wellington or enhance a stuffing or a meat loaf.

TOTAL TIME

2 hours, including cooling time

YIELD

½ cup, enough for about 16 toasts

NUTRITIONAL ANALYSIS PER SERVING

Calories 67.1
Protein 1.3 gm.
Carbohydrates 2.4 gm.
Fat 5.6 gm.
Saturated fat 1.9 gm.
Cholesterol 32.7 mg.
Sodium 59.8 mg.

3 ounces duck fat (from the duck, page 98)

1 large shallot, peeled and coarsely chopped (2½ tablespoons)

1 duck liver (about 3 ounces) (from the duck, page 98), cut into 1-inch pieces

¼ teaspoon *herbes de Provence*

1 clove garlic, peeled and crushed

¼ teaspoon salt

¼ teaspoon freshly ground black pepper

1 teaspoon Cognac

16 ¼-inch-thick horizontal slices from a small baguette, toasted

1 Place the duck fat in a skillet, and cook over medium to high heat for 4 to 5 minutes, until the fat has melted and some of it has browned.

2 Add the shallots, and cook for about 30 seconds, stirring occasionally. Add the liver, *herbes de Provence,* and garlic, and cook over medium to high heat for 1½ to 2 minutes, stirring occasionally. Add the salt and pepper.

3 Transfer the mixture to a blender, add the Cognac, and blend until liquefied. If a finer textured pâté is desired, push the mixture through the holes of a strainer with a spoon. This will yield ½ cup. Let cool for at least 1½ hours, then cover and refrigerate until serving time.

4 Spread the pâté on the toasted baguette slices, and serve. The pâté will keep, well covered and refrigerated, for 3 to 4 days.

Note: If covered with a ½-inch layer of the fat from the cooking of the duck skin (see Mock Peking Duck, page 100), the pâté will keep, refrigerated for up to 2 months. To serve, remove the layer of fat, and consume the pâté within 2 days, refrigerating it between serving times.

Rhubarb and Strawberry Coulis

This dessert unites rhubarb and strawberries, fruits that are especially good when cooked together, as they are here, into a *coulis,* or thick soup. Sweetened with a little sugar and some jam, the *coulis* is beautiful when served in deep plates with a spoonful of sour cream or whipped cream on top and sliced pound cake or cookies on the side.

1½ **pounds ripe rhubarb, trimmed of any greens and root end pieces, washed, and cut into pieces 1 inch across by 3 inches long (4 cups)**

1 **cup ripe strawberries, washed, hulled, and halved or quartered, depending on size**

¾ **cup jam (any type of berry or other fruit, or a mixture of same)**

¼ **cup sugar**

¼ **cup water**

½ **cup sour cream or whipped heavy cream**

Cookies or pound cake

1 Place the rhubarb, strawberries, jam, sugar, and water in a large stainless steel saucepan, and bring to a boil over high heat.

2 Reduce the heat to medium, cover, and cook for 10 minutes, until the fruit is well cooked. Cool to room temperature, and refrigerate until serving time.

3 Ladle into soup plates, and serve each with a rounded tablespoonful of sour cream or whipped cream on top and a few cookies or a slice of pound cake alongside.

TOTAL TIME
20 minutes, plus chiling time

YIELD
4 servings (4 cups)

NUTRITIONAL ANALYSIS PER SERVING

Calories 302.2
Protein 3.1 gm.
Carbohydrates 62.7 gm.
Fat 6.6 gm.
Saturated fat 3.8 gm.
Cholesterol 12.7 mg.
Sodium 46.5 mg.

Cooking Light

A Lean Feast

Steamed Scallops on Spinach
with Walnut Sauce

Corned Beef "Pot-au-feu"

Herbed Yogurt

cheese

Jacques
96

When the temperature begins to rise, and our thoughts turn to summer, beach parties, and how we'll get into last year's bathing suit, it's time to choose leaner foods. This menu is a good place to start.

Occasionally, I find very good buys on scallops at my market, and I suggest you wait until they are reasonably priced where you shop to make the scallop and spinach dish. Since scallops are completely edible, four or five—a total of $^3/_4$ pound—is more than enough to serve four as a first course. I cook the spinach until it begins to wilt in a large stainless steel saucepan, then add the scallops to the pan and steam them along with the spinach for a brief time.

One important advantage of this menu's main course is that the *pot-au-feu* can be prepared ahead in stages. The corned beef can be cooked the morning of the day it will be served—or even, if you are really pressed for time, the day before. The potatoes can be peeled and placed in water to cover, and the other vegetables peeled and trimmed several hours ahead; however, to keep them fresh and beautiful, they should not be added to the pot until about 30 minutes before serving time.

In addition to potatoes, my *pot-au-feu* contains cabbage, onions, turnips, carrots, leeks, and kohlrabi. If you can't find all these vegetables where you live, substitute a like amount of peeled parsnips, sweet potatoes, or chunks of a hard squash.

As main dish garnishes, I serve~along with horseradish and hot Dijon-style mustard~the small, sour French pickles called *cornichons*. My wife, Gloria, makes her own from the small gherkins we grow in our garden each summer, but *cornichons* also are available commercially at specialty food stores.

The low-calorie herbed yogurt cheese, excellent with crunchy country bread, makes a nice finish to this lean meal.

WINES

RED

Kendall Jackson, Grand Reserve,
Zinfandel

WHITE

Macon-Lugny, Les Charmes,
Chardonnay

Special Tip

You can transform leftover *pot-au-feu* into a delicious soup. Shred remaining corned beef, cut the vegetables into small pieces, and combine both with liquid from the stew in a large saucepan (adding chicken stock or water, if necessary, to extend the liquid). Cook briefly, adding a little Cream of Wheat (about 1 tablespoon per cup of liquid) to thicken the mixture, and serve.

Steamed Scallops on Spinach with Walnut Sauce

The beautiful simplicity of this recipe is reflected in its pure, straightforward taste. The ingredients should be of the utmost freshness and quality. Boiling the walnuts beforehand softens them and makes them more like fresh green walnuts, which are more delicate and fruity than the mature walnuts we commonly find in our markets.

TOTAL TIME
About 20 minutes

YIELD
4 servings

NUTRITIONAL ANALYSIS PER SERVING

Calories 267.4
Protein 18.2 gm.
Carbohydrates 7.6 gm.
Fat 19.6 gm.
Saturated fat 2.5 gm.
Cholesterol 28.1 mg.
Sodium 491.2 mg.

WALNUT SAUCE

- 4 **walnuts, shelled, and the nut meats cut into ¼-inch pieces (¼ cup)**
- 2 **tablespoons lemon juice**
- 1 **teaspoon grated lemon rind**
- 4 **tablespoons extra-virgin olive oil**
- ½ **teaspoon salt**
- ½ **teaspoon freshly ground black pepper**

- 1 **pound spinach, tough stems removed (about 14 ounces cleaned)**
- 12 **ounces sea scallops, washed in cool water (16 to 20 scallops)**

1 Bring 2 cups of water to a boil in a small saucepan. Add the walnuts, and bring the water back to a boil. Boil for 30 seconds, and drain. Combine the walnuts in a bowl with the lemon juice, lemon rind, olive oil, salt, and pepper. Mix well, and set aside.

2 At serving time, wash the spinach leaves thoroughly in a basin of cool water, lifting the spinach from the water, and drain in a colander. Place the damp spinach leaves in a large (12-inch) saucepan, and cook over high heat for about 2 minutes, until the spinach starts to steam and wilt.

3 Arrange the scallops on top of the spinach in the saucepan, cover, and cook over high heat for another 3 minutes. By then, the scallops should be just firm and cooked, and the spinach wilted.

Remove the scallops, and place them on a plate. If there is still water remaining in the pan, continue to cook the spinach over high heat, uncovered, for about 1 minute longer, until the moisture is gone.

4 Divide the spinach among four plates, and arrange the scallops on top. Coat with the sauce, and serve immediately.

Corned Beef *Pot-au-Feu*

A classic in French cooking, *pot-au-feu* literally means "pot on the fire" and conventionally consists of boiled beef with an array of vegetables. I use corned beef in my version of this one-pot dish; cured and ready to use right from the market, it is relatively inexpensive when you consider that the meat doesn't require any trimming.

TOTAL TIME
About 3 hours

YIELD
4 servings

NUTRITIONAL ANALYSIS PER SERVING
Calories 429.2
Protein 26.8 gm.
Carbohydrates 29.4 gm.
Fat 22.9 gm.
Saturated fat 7.2 gm.
Cholesterol 81.7 mg.
Sodium 1,919.5 mg.

1   **piece cured (corned) beef, about 2 pounds**

2½ **quarts cold water**

1   **pound red potatoes (about 8), peeled**

1   **small savoy cabbage (1 pound), cut into 6 wedges**

2   **medium onions (8 ounces), peeled**

4   **turnips (12 ounces), peeled**

2   **medium carrots (6 ounces), peeled**

2   **small leeks (8 ounces), trimmed**

2   **kohlrabi (12 ounces), peeled and halved**

2   **bay leaves**

½   **teaspoon dried thyme leaves**

Salt, to taste

GARNISHES
Cornichons
Dijon mustard
Fresh-grated or bottled horseradish

1 Remove the corned beef from the package, and rinse it thoroughly under cool water. Place it in a large pot, and add the cold water.

2 Bring the water to a gentle boil, then skim off and discard any impurities (in the form of foam) that have collected on the surface. Reduce the heat to low, cover, and cook the meat just under the boil or at a very light boil for 2¼ hours.

3 Add the vegetables, herbs, and salt (if needed) to the pot, bring the mixture to a boil, and boil very gently for 30 minutes, or until the vegetables are tender.

4 Remove the meat from the pot, and cut it into thin slices. Remove and discard the bay leaves. Place 3 or 4 slices of corned beef per person in soup plates, and spoon in an assortment of the vegetables and some of the cooking liquid. Pass the *cornichons,* mustard, and horseradish.

Herbed Yogurt Cheese

This is an herbed cheese that I make with yogurt. It is easy and fun to make; you simply drain off the liquid in the yogurt to create a thick cheese. Although this recipe calls for nonfat plain yogurt, you can use a partially defatted or a regular yogurt instead, depending on your own preferences and requirements.

TOTAL TIME
8 hours 15 minutes

YIELD
4 servings

NUTRITIONAL ANALYSIS PER SERVING

Calories 41.7
Protein 4.6 gm.
Carbohydrates 4.6 gm.
Fat 0 gm.
Saturated fat 0 gm.
Cholesterol 0 mg.
Sodium 175.7 mg.

2 **cups nonfat plain yogurt**

1 **scallion, cleaned and finely minced (1 tablespoon)**

1 **tablespoon chopped fresh parsley**

1 **small clove garlic, peeled, crushed, and finely chopped (½ teaspoon)**

¼ **teaspoon freshly ground black pepper**

¼ **teaspoon salt**

Toast, crackers, or bread

1 Place the yogurt in a fine strainer set over a bowl, and refrigerate it for 8 hours to allow the moisture to drain out.

2 Discard the liquid, and place the yogurt in a mixing bowl. Add the scallion, parsley, garlic, pepper, and salt. Mix well.

3 Transfer the mixture to a 12-inch-square piece of cheesecloth. Gather up the edges of the cheesecloth so that the mixture inside forms a ball. Tie the cloth together and refrigerate.

4 When ready to serve, unwrap the cheese, invert onto a plate, and serve with toast, crackers, or regular bread.

Nearly Vegetarian

String bean Ragoût

Swiss Chard-Stuffed Onions

Bulgur and Mint Salad

Pineapple Finale

Jacques 96

Although I am not a vegetarian, my wife and I often prepare very satisfying vegetarian meals. Sometimes, however, we elect to add a small amount of meat to a menu made up primarily of vegetables, fruits, or grains. Such is the case here, where I include sausage–for extra flavor–in my stuffed onion dish.

I begin this meal with a string bean stew. Fresh, good quality, reasonably priced string beans are available almost year-round now at most supermarkets. If the very thin French *haricots verts* are available, use them; if not, select the smallest, thinnest beans you can find. After snapping off the root end of each bean (or, if you like, both ends), cook them in just enough water so that most or all of it will have evaporated by the time the beans are tender–a technique that preserves more of the vegetable's nutrients.

WINE

RED

Edmeades, Pinot Noir

When preparing stuffed onions, I generally use large yellow onions, and especially enjoy Vidalia onions prepared this way. As a stuffing for the onions in this menu, the onion tops and insides are chopped and sautéed along with some chard, garlic, and seasonings. Then, this mixture is combined with crumbled sausage meat.

The salad in this menu is made with bulgur, which is cracked wheat that has been cooked and dried. Good quality bulgur is available inexpensively in health food stores, where it is usually sold loose in barrels. Although it can be cooked again before serving, this is not necessary; bulgur can be reconstituted by merely soaking it in cool tap water for several hours, as I have done for this recipe. Or, if you want to hurry it along, the bulgur can be reconstituted in about half the time by adding it to water that has been brought to a boil. The bulgur should be well drained before it is combined with the other ingredients.

The beautiful and flavorful pineapple dessert that finishes the meal is ideal also for a buffet menu because the presentation is striking and the dish can be prepared beforehand.

CLAUDINE:

~

"I find my friends are talking more about eating a lot of fruits and vegetables. It sounds so *serious. I don't know if it's because society is changing or that people try to eat healthier as they grow older. . . . But, in my house, we've just always had them."*

String Bean Ragoût

After the beans are cooked, spread them out on a platter or cookie sheet to cool while you cook the onion, garlic, tomato, and seasonings together briefly in a saucepan. At serving time, reheat the tomato mixture, add the beans, and warm them through. Serve the ragoût with some crunchy bread.

1½ cups water

1 pound string beans, as thin as possible

1 tablespoon virgin olive oil

1 tablespoon unsalted butter

1 medium onion (about 4 ounces), peeled and coarsely chopped (1 cup)

2 large cloves garlic, peeled and thinly sliced (1 tablespoon)

3 plum tomatoes (about 8 ounces), seeded and cut into 1-inch pieces (about 1 cup)

½ teaspoon salt

¼ teaspoon freshly ground black pepper

1 tablespoon chopped fresh tarragon

1 Place 1¼ cups of the water in a saucepan large enough to hold the beans in one layer, and bring the water to a boil over high heat.

2 Meanwhile, wash the beans, and snap off their root ends. Add the trimmed beans to the boiling water. Cover, and cook over high heat for about 6 to 8 minutes, until the beans are tender and most of the liquid has evaporated. Drain off any remaining liquid, and set the beans aside on a platter or cookie sheet to cool.

3 Meanwhile, heat the oil, butter, onion, and the remaining ¼ cup water in a skillet, and cook over high heat for 5 minutes, or until the water has evaporated and the onion is beginning to fry. Add the garlic, tomatoes, salt, and pepper, and cook for 3 to 4 minutes. Set aside.

4 At serving time, reheat the tomato mixture, then add the beans, and reheat the mixture until the beans are heated through, for 2 to 3 minutes. Sprinkle with the tarragon, and serve immediately.

TOTAL TIME
About 30 minutes

YIELD
4 servings

NUTRITIONAL ANALYSIS PER SERVING
Calories 114.0
Protein 3.0 gm.
Carbohydrates 13.3 gm.
Fat 6.6 gm.
Saturated fat 2.3 gm.
Cholesterol 7.8 mg.
Sodium 286.5 mg.

Swiss Chard-Stuffed Onions

After cooking for about 45 minutes in a hot oven, the onions are soft enough so that the center of each can be removed with a sharp-edged measuring spoon, leaving a receptacle with a wall about ½ inch thick.

TOTAL TIME

2 hours

YIELD

4 servings

NUTRITIONAL ANALYSIS PER SERVING

Calories 417.2
Protein 14.4 gm.
Carbohydrates 34.1 gm.
Fat 26.0 gm.
Saturated fat 7.9 gm.
Cholesterol 45.1 mg.
Sodium 1,005.2 mg.

4 **large onions (about 10 ounces each)**

2 **tablespoons virgin olive oil**

½ **pound Swiss chard, cut into 1-inch pieces, washed, and drained well (4 cups)**

2 **cloves garlic, peeled, crushed, and chopped (2 teaspoons)**

¾ **teaspoon salt**

½ **teaspoon freshly ground black pepper**

½ **pound sweet Italian sausage meat**

2 **tablespoons grated Parmesan cheese**

½ **cup water**

1 Preheat the oven to 425 degrees.

2 Peel the onions, and remove the stem as well as the root end of each. Arrange the onions in one layer on a large piece of aluminum foil, then fold the foil around the onions to enclose them. Place the foil package on a cookie sheet, and bake on the center rack of the 425-degree oven for 45 minutes. The onions should be somewhat soft and partially cooked at this point.

3 Cut a ½-inch slice from the top (stem end) of each onion, and scoop out and reserve the inside to create a receptacle with walls about ½ inch thick. Chop the onion tops and insides coarsely. (You should have about 3½ cups of chopped onion.)

4 Heat the oil until hot but not smoking in a large skillet. Add the chopped onion, and cook for 3 minutes over medium to high heat. Add the Swiss chard, garlic, salt, and pepper, and mix well. Cover, and cook over medium heat for 20 minutes. The mixture should be slightly moist and lightly browned. Let cool to lukewarm, then mix in the sausage meat.

5 Stuff the onions with the chard and sausage mixture, dividing it evenly among them and mounding it so that all the stuffing is used.

6 Arrange the stuffed onions in a gratin dish, and sprinkle them with the Parmesan.

7 Pour the water around the onions in the gratin dish, and bake at 400 degrees for 60 minutes, until brown on top and very soft throughout.

Bulgur and Mint Salad

I especially like Tabasco sauce, and have used it liberally in the salad because I think its hotness contrasts nicely with the coolness and pungency of the mint and other herbs. Light and delightful, this summer dish can be served as a first course or as an accompaniment to almost any meat or fish main course. It will keep, refrigerated, for four or five days.

TOTAL TIME
4 hours

YIELD
4 servings

NUTRITIONAL ANALYSIS PER SERVING

Calories 277.4
Protein 5.9 gm.
Carbohydrates 34.9 gm.
Fat 14.4 gm.
Saturated fat 1.8 gm.
Cholesterol 0 mg.
Sodium 590.0 mg.

1 cup bulgur wheat

1 cup lightly packed mint leaves

1 cup lightly packed fresh parsley or other herbs

1 carrot (about 5 ounces), peeled and grated into strips using the large-hole side of a cheese grater (about ½ cup)

4 scallions, cleaned and minced (about ⅓ cup)

2 to 3 cloves garlic, peeled, crushed, and minced (about 2 teaspoons)

1 teaspoon salt

¾ teaspoon Tabasco hot pepper sauce (less if you prefer milder seasonings)

¼ cup lemon juice

¼ cup corn oil

1 Place the bulgur in a bowl, and add about 3 cups cool water. Soak for at least 3 to 4 hours, or as long as overnight.

2 Meanwhile, coarsely chop the mint and parsley together. (You should have 1 cup.)

3 Drain the bulgur in a sieve for 10 to 20 minutes. Place the drained bulgur in a bowl, and add the remaining ingredients. Mix well.

4 Serve at room temperature.

Pineapple Finale

"Ripe" is the key word here; if your pineapple isn't ripe, this dessert isn't worth making. Select fruit that is slightly soft to the touch and has a pleasant, fruity smell.

1 ripe pineapple, with top and leaves intact (about 4 pounds)

½ cup orange juice

2 tablespoons honey

2 tablespoons pear brandy

1 Make a crosswise cut about 1 inch below the top of the body of the pineapple, removing the leaves and top of the fruit. Reserve this pineapple top and leaves. Cut a ½-inch slice from the bottom of the pineapple.

2 Place the pineapple on its side, push the sharp blade of a flexible knife into the flesh of the pineapple as close as possible to where the flesh meets the shell, and cut all around the flesh until you can remove intact a cylinder of pure pineapple flesh. Reserve the hollowed-out pineapple shell.

3 Cut the pineapple flesh crosswise into 8 slices of about equal thickness, and, using a small round cookie cutter or sharp knife, remove the tough center (about 1¼ inches in diameter) from each slice.

4 Stack the slices in the order in which they were cut, and place them back in the shell. Set the reassembled pineapple in a glass serving bowl.

5 Mix the orange juice, honey, and brandy together in a small bowl, and pour it over the pineapple. Refrigerate the dessert, covered, until serving time. The recipe can be completed to this point up to 8 hours ahead.

6 At serving time, place the reserved pineapple top with leaves on top of the re-formed pineapple, and bring the dessert to the table. Serve two slices of pineapple per person with some of the surrounding juice.

TOTAL TIME
15 minutes, plus chilling time

YIELD
4 servings

NUTRITIONAL ANALYSIS PER SERVING
Calories 182.5
Protein 1.2 gm.
Carbohydrates 43.6 gm.
Fat 1.0 gm.
Saturated fat 0.1 gm.
Cholesterol 0 mg.
Sodium 3.1 mg.

Meatless Summer Supper

Little corn dumplings

Cold Corn Soup

Mixed Vegetable Salad with toasted bread Cubes

Plums "au Sucre"

This refreshing vegetarian menu is a salute to summer. Loaded with vegetables and fruit, the meal takes advantage of the bounty of the season.

If you prefer your soups a bit chunkier, the corn soup ingredients can be used to create a corn bisque. To do so, sauté the onion as directed in step 1 of the recipe. Then combine it with the potatoes, salt, and water, and cook the mixture for 20 to 30 minutes, or until the potatoes are tender. Puree this mixture in a food processor, transfer it to a saucepan, and add the whole corn kernels. Bring to a boil, and boil for a few seconds. Add the milk and chives or tarragon, and serve immediately.

For my mixed vegetable salad, I love the small French *haricots verts*, those very thin string beans. If they aren't available, take a little extra time, and sort through the loose beans at the market, seeking out specimens that are plump and firm, but small. Because they are younger, the smaller beans are a bit more tender. I cook them in a skillet with just enough unsalted water so that by the time the beans are cooked, most of the water has evaporated.

This cooking procedure prevents the loss of valuable nutrients that used to be a common occurrence when vegetables were cooked in large amounts of water, especially since the water was drained off and discarded (along with the nutrients) when the vegetables were done. We don't refresh the beans here either—another standard practice in the past that contributed to nutrient loss.

The zucchini for the salad is steamed for only a few minutes, so it is still quite firm. The romaine can, of course, be replaced by another type of lettuce, perhaps escarole or curly endive, both of which hold a dressing well and remain crunchy. Either regular or plum tomatoes can be used in the salad—select whichever variety is most ripe, but make sure the tomatoes are firm enough so the cubes retain their shape. This combination salad is conventionally tossed at the last moment and can be served with extra bread, if desired.

WINES

WHITE

Springbok, Chardonnay

RED

Dôle du Valais, Swiss Wine

For dessert, I prepare a simple mixture of plums flavored with sugar and lemon juice. As an optional accompaniment, cookies can be served with the plums and a little dollop of sour cream or yogurt placed alongside them. I use Santa Rosa plums here, but substitute the large Friar plums or another similar type if they are of better quality at your market.

Little Corn Dumplings

These little corn dumplings are a bonus, a treat I make when I'm already buying corn for recipes like the one in this menu for cold corn soup. I usually serve the dumplings with an apéritif or drinks before the meal or as an accompaniment for the soup.

TOTAL TIME
About 15 minutes

YIELD
4 servings

NUTRITIONAL ANALYSIS PER SERVING
Calories 212.0
Protein 4.5 gm.
Carbohydrates 23.0 gm.
Fat 12.2 gm.
Saturated fat 1.2 gm.
Cholesterol 53.1 mg.
Sodium 282.3 mg.

⅓ cup all-purpose flour

2 tablespoons cornstarch

1 teaspoon baking powder

¼ teaspoon salt

1 egg

⅓ cup ice water

2 ears sweet corn, husked and kernels removed (1½ cups)

6 tablespoons canola oil, for cooking the dumplings

1 Mix the flour, cornstarch, baking powder, and half the salt together in a bowl. Add the egg and ¼ cup of the water, and mix with a whisk until smooth. Add the remainder of the water, and mix until smooth. Fold in the corn kernels.

2 Heat 3 tablespoons of the oil in a large (12-inch) skillet, and drop 1 tablespoon of batter into the skillet for each dumpling, cooking about 10 dumplings at one time over medium to high heat for 3 to 4 minutes on each side. Transfer the dumplings to a wire rack when they are cooked, and repeat with the remaining batter and oil.

3 Sprinkle the dumplings with the remaining salt, and serve immediately. (Alternatively, prepare a few hours ahead, and reheat on the wire rack set over a cookie sheet in a 375-degree oven for 10 to 15 minutes.)

Cold Corn Soup

This corn soup can be served hot as well as cold. It consists simply of onion, corn kernels, and potatoes—which act as a thickening agent—cooked together in water, then pureed in a food processor, and, finally, finished with milk and chopped chives to create a type of corn vichyssoise. One advantage of this soup is that it can be made ahead; it will keep, refrigerated, for four or five days (in that case, however, I would not add the milk until just before it is served).

1	tablespoon unsalted butter
1	tablespoon corn oil
1	medium onion (6 ounces), peeled and sliced (about 1¾ cups)
½	pound potatoes, peeled and cut into 2-inch chunks
4	large ears corn, husked and kernels removed (3½ cups)
1	teaspoon salt
2½	cups water
1½	cups cold milk
2	tablespoons chopped fresh chives or fresh tarragon

1 Heat the butter and oil in a large saucepan. Add the sliced onion, and sauté it for 2 minutes. Mix in the potatoes, corn kernels, salt, and water. Bring the mixture to a boil, cover, reduce the heat to low, and boil gently for 30 minutes.

2 Using a hand blender, puree the soup in the saucepan; alternatively, transfer the soup to the bowl of a food processor, and process until pureed. Then, for soup with a smoother, finer texture, push it through a fine sieve set over a mixing bowl. Stir in the cold milk and chives or tarragon. Refrigerate until serving time.

Variation: To serve the soup hot: After pureeing in step 2, add the milk to the soup in the saucepan and bring the mixture to a boil. Mix in the chives or tarragon, and serve.

TOTAL TIME
45 minutes

YIELD
4 servings

NUTRITIONAL ANALYSIS PER SERVING
Calories 276.2
Protein 8.7 gm.
Carbohydrates 41.0 gm.
Fat 11.0 gm.
Saturated fat 4.4 gm.
Cholesterol 20.6 mg.
Sodium 619.7 mg.

Mixed Vegetable Salad with Toasted Bread Cubes

This salad consists of string beans, zucchini, tomatoes, and romaine lettuce, all tossed in a garlicky dressing and garnished with large croutons made from leftover bread. My preference is for country-style, earthy bread, which I cut into chunks, then brown in the oven. Added to the salad a few minutes before it is served, these cubes absorb a little of the dressing and soften slightly while still retaining their crunch. If you want your croutons to be even softer, toss the salad a bit earlier—15 to 20 minutes before serving it.

TOTAL TIME
20 minutes

YIELD
4 servings

NUTRITIONAL ANALYSIS PER SERVING

Calories 230.0
Protein 4.9 gm.
Carbohydrates 22.1 gm.
Fat 15.1 gm.
Saturated fat 2.2 gm.
Cholesterol 0 mg.
Sodium 418.7 mg.

- 1 cup plus 2 tablespoons water
- ½ pound very thin string beans (preferably *haricots verts*), tips removed
- ½ pound zucchini, washed and cut into ¾-inch pieces (2 cups)
- 3 ounces baguette or other leftover bread (preferably from a French country-style loaf), cut into 1- to 1½-inch cubes
- 2 regular tomatoes or 5 or 6 plum tomatoes (¾ pound), cut into 1-inch pieces (about 2½ cups)
- ½ head romaine lettuce (about 5 ounces), cut into 2-inch pieces, washed, and thoroughly dried (5 cups)

DRESSING

- 2 cloves garlic, peeled, crushed, and finely chopped (1 teaspoon)
- 2 tablespoons red wine vinegar
- 4 tablespoons extra-virgin olive oil
- ½ teaspoon salt
- ⅓ teaspoon freshly ground black pepper

1. Preheat the oven to 400 degrees.

2. Bring 1 cup of the water to a boil in a skillet. Add the beans, and cook them over medium to high heat, covered, until tender, about 6 minutes. Drain off any remaining water. Place the beans in a large serving bowl.

3. Place the remaining 2 tablespoons water in the same skillet. Add the zucchini pieces, and cook them, covered, over high heat for 2 minutes. (The zucchini should have softened a little, and the water should have evaporated.) Add the zucchini to the bowl containing the beans.

4. Arrange the baguette pieces in one layer on a baking sheet, and place in the 400-degree oven until brown, about 8 minutes. Set the croutons aside.

5. Add the tomato pieces and the salad greens to the beans and zucchini in the bowl. In a separate bowl, mix the dressing ingredients.

6. At serving time, add the browned bread pieces and the dressing to the salad mixture in the bowl. Mix well.

Plums au Sucre

This simple dessert combines wedges of plum with lemon juice and sugar. The mixture is set aside—with an occasional stirring—to macerate for about an hour before serving. In fact, the dish could be assembled a few hours ahead. Serve the plums cool but not cold.

TOTAL TIME
10 minutes, plus chilling time

YIELD
4 servings

NUTRITIONAL ANALYSIS PER SERVING

Calories 149.2
Protein 1.5 gm.
Carbohydrates 27.7gm.
Fat 4.7 gm.
Saturated fat 2.5 gm.
Cholesterol 8.3 mg.
Sodium 11.8 mg.

6 to 8 Santa Rosa plums (or another variety), well ripened (1 pound)

2 tablespoons lemon juice

¼ cup sugar

1 tablespoon plum brandy (Mirabelle or Quetsche), or another fruit brandy, like pear or cherry (kirsch) (optional)

⅓ cup sour cream

Cookies (optional)

1 Wash the plums, and cut them in half. Discard the pits, and cut each half plum into thirds. Place the plum pieces in a bowl.

2 Add the lemon juice, sugar, and brandy, if desired, to the plums, and mix well. Cover with plastic wrap, and refrigerate for at least 1 hour but as long as 6 hours.

3 Spoon the plums and surrounding juice into wineglasses or onto dessert plates, and serve with a dollop of sour cream and cookies, if desired.

Apple & Carrot Salad
with yogurt
Tomato chowder with
Mollet eggs and croûtons
Cheese wafer crisps
Grapefruit Gratin

After the Holidays

Jacques 96

After the holidays, a special weekend, or other occasions when I have overindulged, I crave simple, lean dishes like those in this menu.

We begin with an apple and carrot salad with yogurt. Low-fat yogurt can be used here, if you like., Since the salad contains no vinegar or fat, it is very light and wholesome.

WINE

WHITE

Conte D'Attimis-Maniago, Pinot Grigio

The main course is a soup, its chowder base a harmonious blend of vegetables—onions, carrots, scallions, garlic, and fresh and canned tomatoes. I use fresh cherry tomatoes here, often finding them more flavorful than regular tomatoes early in the season, and canned plum tomatoes, which are usually tasty. If you have access to a large supply of fresh, ripe tomatoes in full summer, eliminate the canned ones altogether, and make the soup with fresh tomatoes only. A mollet egg is placed in each bowl of soup at serving time, along with a crouton, preferably made from a large, crusty, country-style loaf of bread. Although optional, cheese wafer crisps make a tasty addition to the chowder.

I enjoy grapefruit in almost any form but particularly like it served as it is in this menu—segmented, sprinkled with brown sugar, and broiled until warmed through and lightly browned. Wonderfully refreshing, it's a perfect ending to this and almost any meal.

Apple and Carrot Salad with Yogurt

Assemble this salad a couple of hours ahead to allow the carrots to soften and the dish to develop more flavor.

TOTAL TIME

15 minutes, plus
about 2 hours
cooling time

YIELD

4 servings

NUTRITIONAL ANALYSIS PER SERVING

Calories 94.8
Protein 2.1 gm.
Carbohydrates 19.3 gm.
Fat 1.8 gm.
Saturated fat 0.9 gm.
Cholesterol 5.5 mg.
Sodium 172.6 mg.

¾ **cup plain yogurt**

1 **tablespoon red wine vinegar**

¼ **teaspoon freshly ground black pepper**

¼ **teaspoon salt**

3 **tablespoons chopped fresh cilantro**

3 **carrots (8 ounces), peeled and shredded (3½ cups)**

2 **apples (12 ounces), left unpeeled and cut into ¼-inch sticks (2½ cups) (see Note)**

Lettuce leaves

Crusty French bread

1 Combine the yogurt, vinegar, pepper, salt, and cilantro in a bowl. Add the carrots and apples, and mix well. Cover, and refrigerate for a few hours to soften the carrot slightly.

2 Spoon the salad onto lettuce leaves, and serve with crusty bread.

Note: To prepare the unpeeled apples, stand them upright on a cutting board. Starting on one side, cut each apple vertically into ¼-inch slices, stopping when you reach the core, pivoting the apple, and cutting again, until only the core remains. Then discard the cores, stack the apple slices together, and cut them into ¼-inch sticks.

Cheese Wafer Crisps

These simple wafers couldn't be easier to make. Be sure to use a nonstick skillet and cook the wafers over medium heat. Broken into pieces, they make an excellent garnish for soup, salad, or even sautéed fish.

4 tablespoons grated Parmesan cheese (preferably Parmigiano-Reggiano)

1 Heat a 6-inch nonstick skillet until warm. Sprinkle 1 tablespoon of the grated cheese in the skillet to create a wafer about 4 inches in diameter. Cook over medium heat for about 2 to 2½ minutes, until the cheese is lightly browned throughout.

2 Remove the pan from the heat, and let the wafer cool and firm up for 20 to 30 seconds before removing it carefully with a flat spatula. Repeat with the remaining cheese, making 3 additional wafers.

3 Serve the wafers whole, or break them into pieces. Use as a garnish on salad, soup, or other dishes to your liking.

TOTAL TIME
5 minutes

YIELD
4 wafers

NUTRITIONAL ANALYSIS PER SERVING
Calories 19.4
Protein 1.6 gm.
Carbohydrates 0 gm.
Fat 1.4 gm.
Saturated fat 1.1 gm.
Cholesterol 4.4 mg.
Sodium 31.8 mg.

Tomato Chowder with Mollet Eggs and Croutons

This basic tomato soup, served with mollet eggs and large croutons made from stale country-style bread, can be made totally vegetarian by replacing the chicken stock with vegetable stock or water.

A French favorite, mollet eggs are similar to poached eggs in texture, with runny yolks and soft whites. This result is achieved by cooking eggs in their shells in barely boiling water to cover for 4 to 5 minutes, depending on their size, then thoroughly cooling and carefully shelling them.

TOTAL TIME
About 1 hour

YIELD
4 servings

NUTRITIONAL ANALYSIS PER SERVING
Calories 329.3
Protein 13.4 gm.
Carbohydrates 34.5 gm.
Fat 16.2 gm.
Saturated fat 3.5 gm.
Cholesterol 189.8 mg.
Sodium 1,040.5 mg.

2 tablespoons virgin olive oil

1 medium onion (6 ounces), peeled and coarsely chopped (1¼ cups)

6 scallions, trimmed (but with green left on) and chopped (¾ cup)

1 carrot, peeled and coarsely chopped (½ cup)

3 cloves garlic, peeled, crushed, and chopped (2 teaspoons)

2 tablespoons all-purpose flour

3 cups chicken stock, preferably homemade unsalted and defatted, or 3 cups water and 1 chicken bouillon cube

12 ounces cherry tomatoes

1 (15-ounce) can plum tomatoes, preferably imported

1 teaspoon salt

½ teaspoon freshly ground black pepper

1 teapoon dried thyme leaves

¼ teaspoon dried sage leaves

GARNISHES

4 slices country-style bread (4 ounces), preferably stale, for croutons

2 teaspoons virgin olive oil

1 small clove garlic, peeled

4 medium eggs

½ cup grated Swiss cheese (optional)

1 Heat the 2 tablespoons olive oil in a large, sturdy saucepan. When the oil is hot but not smoking, add the onion, scallions, carrot, and chopped garlic, and cook over high heat, stirring constantly, for 6 to 8 minutes. Sprinkle the flour on top of the mixture, stir thoroughly, and cook for 2 minutes longer, stirring. Mix in the stock.

2 Meanwhile, place the cherry tomatoes in the bowl of a food processor and process until coarsely chopped. (You should have about 1½ cups.) Add the can of plum tomatoes and process for 5 seconds. Add to the soup with the salt, pepper, thyme, and sage. Bring to a boil, stirring occasionally, then cover, reduce the heat to low, and cook for 25 to 30 minutes.

3 Preheat the oven to 400 degrees.

4 While the soup is cooking, *prepare the garnishes:* Brush the bread slices with the 2 teaspoons olive oil, and bake them in a single layer on a cookie sheet in the 400-degree oven for 10 to 12 minutes, or until nicely browned. Rub one side of the croutons with the

peeled garlic clove, and set them aside.

5 Using a thumbtack or pushpin, make a hole in the rounded end of each egg. Lower the eggs gently into a pan containing enough boiling water to cover them, and cook the eggs for 4 to 5 minutes in barely boiling water. Drain the hot water from the pan, and shake the pan to crack the shells of the eggs on all sides. Fill the pan with ice and water, and set the eggs aside to cool completely.

6 When the eggs are cool, peel them carefully (so as not to damage the yolks, which are still runny) under cool running water.

7 At serving time, bring the soup to a strong boil, and ladle about 10 ounces of it into each of four bowls. Place an egg in the center of each bowl, and wait for about 5 minutes for the eggs to warm in the center. Place a crouton in each bowl, and serve, sprinkled, if desired, with the cheese.

CLAUDINE:
~

"After the holidays (when I've been eating like there's no tomorrow), for some reason I really love broccoli rabe. It's kind of cleansing and purifying. I'm also drawn to soup, green vegetables (any kind), and Honey Nut Cheerios. The last thing you want after the holidays is a steak."

Grapefruit Gratin

This easy, flavorful dessert can be prepared ahead up to the cooking step. This is best done at the last moment so that the grapefruit sections are warm, soft, and slightly caramelized on top when consumed.

TOTAL TIME
15 minutes

YIELD
4 servings

NUTRITIONAL ANALYSIS PER SERVING

Calories 98.9
Protein 0.7 gm.
Carbohydrates 18.7 gm.
Fat 3.0 gm.
Saturated fat 1.8 gm.
Cholesterol 7.8 mg.
Sodium 4.4 mg.

2 **grapefruits, preferably pink, about 1 pound each**

3 **tablespoons light brown sugar**

1 **tablespoon unsalted butter**

1 **tablespoon Cognac (optional)**

1 Using a sharp, thin-bladed knife, remove the skin and underlying cottony pith from each grapefruit, leaving the fruit totally exposed. Then cut between the membranes on each side of the grapefruit segments, and remove the flesh in wedgelike pieces. You should have about 24 sections of grapefruit in all. Squeeze the membranes over a bowl to extract the juice, and drink this at your leisure.

2 Arrange the grapefruit sections in one layer in a gratin dish. When ready to serve them, preheat the broiler.

3 Sprinkle the grapefruit with the sugar, and dot them with the butter. Place about 4 inches under the broiler, and broil for 8 to 10 minutes, or until the edges of the segments are lightly browned. If desired, sprinkle with the Cognac, and serve immediately.

Menus for Special Occasions

Here is a rich, elegant, and complex menu that will give you a boost when the stakes are high~for instance, when you are courting an important client or angling for a raise or a promotion. Invite the client or your boss home for this wonderful dinner, and it's more than likely that your efforts will be rewarded.

The first course is an attractive *gâteau*. The polenta and vegetables are cooked and then layered in a mold. When set and unmolded, the ribbons of color created by the vegetable layers make this dish as beautiful as it is delicious.

Despite the fact that the escalopes of veal are easy and take practically no time at all to make, this is an elegant main course that is sure to impress your special guests.

WINES

WHITE

Michele Chiarlo, Gavi

RED

Paul Jaboulet, Hermitage La Chapelle

I serve the veal with a side dish of carrot crêpes. You can experiment by substituting a puree of peas for the carrots, creating flavorful green pancakes.

The dessert is a *clafoutis,* a type of thickened custard. Unlike a conventional custard, which is usually cooked in a double boiler, the *clafoutis*~made here with delicious fresh strawberries~is baked in a gratin dish.

Polenta and Vegetable *Gâteau*

This *gâteau,* or molded "cake," makes an unusual and stunning garnish for a roast, or it can be served—as it is here—as the first course of a special meal. The stock obtained from cooking vegetables for the dish is used to cook and flavor polenta, the Northern Italian staple made from cornmeal. A tomato sauce, spooned over the *gâteau,* adds more color to the eye-catching display.

Feel free to experiment with whatever vegetables you have on hand.

TOTAL TIME
About 30 minutes

YIELD
4 servings

NUTRITIONAL ANALYSIS PER SERVING
Calories 220.1
Protein 5.4 gm.
Carbohydrates 29.7 gm.
Fat 9.8 gm.
Saturated fat 1.3 gm.
Cholesterol 0 mg.
Sodium 862.0 mg.

- 2 **tablespoons virgin olive oil**
- 3 **cups water, plus additional as needed**
- 1½ **teaspoons salt**
- 2 **ounces snow peas, cleaned, with ends and strings removed (⅔ cup)**
- 1 **carrot (4 ounces), peeled and cut into strips with a vegetable peeler (1 cup)**
- 4 **ounces trimmed spinach (tough stems removed), washed (about 2½ cups loose)**
- ½ **cup chopped onion**
- 2 **tablespoons pignoli nuts**
- 8 **ounces cherry tomatoes, quartered (1½ cups)**
- ¼ **teaspoon freshly ground black pepper**
- ¾ **cup yellow cornmeal**

1 Oil a 6-cup measuring cup or medium bowl with a little of the olive oil, and set it aside.

2 Bring the 3 cups water to a boil in a medium saucepan, and add 1 teaspoon of the salt. Add the snow peas, bring the water back to a boil, and boil the peas for 2½ minutes. Using a slotted spoon, remove the peas from the water, and place them in a small bowl. Toss the peas with ⅛ teaspoon of the salt and 1 teaspoon of the olive oil, and set them aside.

3 To the boiling water in the saucepan, add the carrot strips, bring the water back to a boil, and boil for 1 minute. Using a skimmer, remove the carrots from the water, and place them in a small bowl. Toss the carrots with ⅛ teaspoon of the salt and

1 teaspoon of the olive oil, and set them aside. Measure the vegetable cooking liquid and add enough water so that you have 3 cups.

4 Place 1 teaspoon of the olive oil in a medium skillet, and add the spinach (still wet from washing) with ⅛ teaspoon of the salt. Cook over medium to high heat for 1 minute, covered, until the spinach is wilted. Transfer the spinach to a bowl, and set it aside.

5 For the tomato sauce: Place the rest of the olive oil (about 1 tablespoon) in a skillet, add the onion and pignoli nuts, and sauté for 1 minute. Add the tomatoes, the remaining ⅛ teaspoon salt, and the pepper, and cook for 2 to 3 minutes, until the tomatoes are wilted. Set aside.

6 To cook the cornmeal, add the yellow cornmeal to the saucepan with the reserved hot vegetable cooking liquid, mixing it well with a whisk as you do so to prevent caking and lumping. Bring the mixture to a boil, cover, reduce the heat to very low, and cook for 5 minutes, stirring occasionally with the whisk.

7 Preheat the oven to 180 degrees.

8 Place about ¼ of the polenta in the oiled cup or bowl, and arrange the spinach on top to create a second layer. Add another layer of polenta, then spoon in the carrots. Add yet another layer of polenta, and spoon the snow peas on top. Finish with the rest of the polenta. Cover with a plate, and let rest for 10 to 15 minutes to set the polenta.

9 When the polenta is set, turn the *gâteau* upside down on a plate, leaving the cup or bowl in place over it. Keep warm in the 180-degree oven until ready to serve (up to 1 hour). Unmold the *gâteau,* spoon some of the tomato mixture over it, and serve. Eat with a spoon.

CLAUDINE:

~

"Food can create a lot of moods, one of which is elegance and refinement. There are different ways you can present yourself through the food you make. I think it's really nice sometimes to make a meal that's a little more elegant and sophisticated, and kind of classical."

Escalopes of Veal in Mushroom and Cognac Sauce

This elegant dish is the quickest to prepare on this menu, which makes it ideal for many other occasions, too—even when company comes on short notice. If you want to cut down on the calories, you can omit the cream and just complete the dish as instructed.

TOTAL TIME
10 minutes

YIELD
4 servings

NUTRITIONAL ANALYSIS PER SERVING
Calories 312.1
Protein 26.1 gm.
Carbohydrates 4.6 gm.
Fat 19.5 gm.
Saturated fat 9.8 gm.
Cholesterol 137.0 mg.
Sodium 638.3 mg.

1 tablespoon unsalted butter

1 tablespoon peanut oil

8 thin slices (scaloppine) of veal (each about ½ inch thick), about 1 pound total

1 teaspoon salt

2 tablespoons chopped shallots

2 tablespoons dry, fruity white wine

1 tablespoon Cognac

8 ounces button mushrooms, washed just before cooking

½ cup heavy cream

¼ teaspoon freshly ground black pepper

2 teaspoons lemon juice

1 teaspoon chopped fresh chives

1 Preheat the oven to 170 degrees.

2 Divide the butter and oil between two skillets, each 8 to 10 inches in diameter. Sprinkle the veal with ½ teaspoon of the salt. Heat the butter and oil until very hot, then add the veal to the skillets in one layer, and cook it over high heat for 45 seconds to 1 minute on each side. Using a spatula, transfer the veal to an ovenproof dish, and place it in the 170-degree oven to keep warm while you complete the dish.

3 Add the shallots to one of the skillets, and sauté for 30 seconds. Add the wine, and stir well to melt all the solidified juices in the skillet. Then pour the contents of that skillet into the second skillet, and add the Cognac and mushrooms. Bring to a boil over high heat, cover, and cook over

medium to high heat for 5 minutes. (Initially liquid will come out of the mushrooms, but after 5 minutes all but 2 or 3 tablespoons of the liquid will have evaporated.)

4 Add the cream, the remaining salt, and the pepper. Bring to a

boil, and boil for 30 seconds. Stir in the lemon juice.

5 Arrange two veal escalopes on each plate, and coat the veal with the sauce and mushrooms. Top with the chives, and serve immediately.

"Veal is always a kind of celebration. With Cognac and mushroom sauce, it takes on this beautiful, traditional elegance."

Carrot Crêpes

These delicate and delicious crêpes are served as a side dish here, but are appealing also as a first course or a garnish for meat or fish. Although the crêpes are best when just out of the skillet, they can be made ahead, laid out in one layer on a cookie sheet or tray, and reheated in a 300-degree oven until warmed through.

3 **carrots (12 ounces), peeled and cut into 2-inch pieces**

1½ **cups water**

1 **tablespoon cornstarch**

1 **tablespoon all-purpose flour**

½ **teaspoon salt**

¼ **teaspoon freshly ground black pepper**

¼ **teaspoon sugar**

¼ **cup milk**

2 **eggs**

2 **tablespoons finely minced scallion greens (the green top of 1 scallion)**

3 **tablespoons canola oil**

1 Place the carrots in a saucepan with the water. Bring to a boil over high heat, cover, reduce the heat to low, and boil gently for 18 to 20 minutes, until the carrots are fork-tender and all but about 2 tablespoons of the cooking liquid has evaporated.

2 Place the carrots and cooking liquid in the bowl of a food processor, and process for 10 to 15 seconds. Add the cornstarch, flour, salt, pepper, sugar, and milk, and process for a few seconds. Add the eggs, and process until very smooth. Pour into a bowl, and stir in the minced scallions.

3 To cook, heat 1 tablespoon of the oil in a 10-inch nonstick skillet. When the oil is hot, add about 2 tablespoons of the carrot mixture per crêpe, and cook about 4 crêpes at a time over medium heat for 2 minutes. Using a flat metal spatula, turn the crêpes over, and cook them for 2 minutes on the other side. Repeat with the remaining oil and batter.

4 Serve immediately, or set aside for up to 1 hour, and then reheat in a 300-degree oven before serving.

TOTAL TIME
40 minutes

YIELD
About 12 crêpes

NUTRITIONAL ANALYSIS PER SERVING
Calories 61.9
Protein 1.5 gm.
Carbohydrates 4.1 gm.
Fat 4.4 gm.
Saturated fat 0.6 gm.
Cholesterol 36.1 mg.
Sodium 113.1 mg.

Strawberry Clafoutis

Strawberries are used here in a *clafoutis,* a type of thickened custard usually reserved for cherries (which can be substituted here for the strawberries, as can other types of berries). I use a little cornstarch as a thickening agent, combining it with eggs, sugar, milk, vanilla, and the berries.

TOTAL TIME
45 minutes

YIELD
4 servings

NUTRITIONAL ANALYSIS PER SERVING

Calories 182.6
Protein 6.6 gm.
Carbohydrates 26.0 gm.
Fat 5.9 gm.
Saturated fat 2.7 gm.
Cholesterol 119.1 mg.
Sodium 77.5 mg.

¼ **cup sugar**

1 **tablespoon cornstarch**

1½ **teaspoons pure vanilla extract**

2 **eggs**

1½ **cups milk**

1½ **cups strawberries (about 10 ounces), cleaned and hulled**

1 **teaspoon confectioners' sugar**

1 Preheat the oven to 350 degrees.

2 Mix the sugar and cornstarch in a bowl. Add the vanilla and eggs, and mix well with a whisk for 30 to 40 seconds. Add the milk, and mix until it is incorporated.

3 Quarter the berries and distribute them evenly in a 4- to 6-cup gratin dish.

4 Pour the egg mixture over the berries, and place the gratin dish on a cookie sheet. Bake the gratin in the 350-degree oven for about 40 minutes, until just set. Cool to room temperature.

5 Sprinkle confectioners' sugar on top of the cool gratin, and serve at room temperature.

A Family Celebration

Artichoke and Tomato Stew

Poached Salmon in "Ravigote" Sauce

Green Couscous

Chocolate Paris-Brest

Jacques '96

"I started drinking wine when I was very young. I'd have a glass of water, and my parents would add a little red wine, so that if you held the glass up to the light, you'd just see a tiny tinge of red. As I got older, the wine increased and the water decreased— until, when I was eighteen, I was permitted to have a glass of wine at the table. We've always enjoyed wine in my family."

This tasty and showy menu is meant to please and to satisfy. It will also impress special guests because each dish reflects qualities of the cook: the artichoke dish demonstrates a knowledge of basic knife skills; the salmon main dish exhibits an understanding of how to properly poach fish; the couscous side dish reveals an awareness of the importance of timing in meal preparation, so that dishes that are to be served together are ready at the same time; and the Paris-Brest cake shows a willingness to learn pastry-making techniques and master dessert cream preparations.

The tips of artichoke leaves have thorny prickers, so the vegetables must be carefully trimmed for the first-course stew. Make sure you have a good, sharp knife. Although this process (described in detail in step 1, page 158) may take you a few minutes, it is well worth the

W I N E S

W H I T E

Lakewood, Sauvignon Blanc

D E S S E R T   W I N E

Muscat de Saint Jean de Minervois

effort, since everything that remains is edible. Cooked with tomato, onion, and garlic, this dish also can be served as an accompaniment to meat or poultry.

Most salmon sold today is farm-raised, so it is of uniformly good quality. When production in numerous countries~from Chile to Canada and elsewhere in the world~is up, the price tends to drop substantially, and that's when you should take advantage of the market.

Special Tip

Salmon freezes well, so buy it (super fresh!) at your fish store or supermarket when it is attractively priced, remove the skin, cut it into steaks, double wrap, and freeze. When ready to use, defrost under refrigeration, still wrapped, so it doesn't dry out.

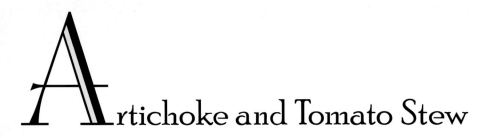 rtichoke and Tomato Stew

In peak condition, artichokes can be costly—sometimes more than a dollar each. When they begin to yellow a little, however, five or six of them are usually packaged together at my market and sold at a very reasonable price. This is when I buy artichokes for artichoke bottom recipes or for stews.

TOTAL TIME

35 minutes

YIELD

4 servings

NUTRITIONAL ANALYSIS PER SERVING

Calories 120.9
Protein 3.2 gm.
Carbohydrates 13.7 gm.
Fat 7.2 gm.
Saturated fat 1.0 gm.
Cholesterol 0 mg.
Sodium 341.0 mg.

4　medium artichokes (about 5 to 6 ounces each)

2　tablespoons virgin olive oil

2　medium tomatoes (12 ounces total), cut into 1-inch pieces (3 cups)

1　medium onion (4 ounces), peeled and thinly sliced (¾ cup)

2　large garlic cloves, peeled and thinly sliced (1 tablespoon)

½　teaspoon salt

½　teaspoon freshly ground black pepper

½　cup water, plus additional as needed

1　With a sharp knife, cut 1½ inches from the top of each artichoke. Then trim off the tough outer leaves of the artichokes with the knife, taking care that you don't cut into the tender inner leaves or the white heart inside. If your artichokes have stems, peel off the outer layer of these to make them edible. Quarter the trimmed artichokes, and remove and discard the bristly choke from each piece.

2　Place the artichokes in a saucepan (preferably stainless steel), and add the rest of the ingredients. Bring to a strong boil over high heat, then lower the heat to medium-low, cover, and cook for 20 minutes, or until the artichokes are moist and tender when pricked with a kitchen fork. Add a few additional tablespoons of water at the end of the cooking period if the mixture appears dry.

3　Cool to room temperature, and serve.

Poached Salmon in *Ravigote* Sauce

Salmon fillet steaks are poached here very briefly, then served with a *ravigote* sauce. *Ravigote* means "to invigorate" in French, and this sauce, containing tomatoes, scallions, garlic, parsley, lemon juice, and olive oil, awakens the taste buds and complements the salmon perfectly.

I also have added pickled capers to the sauce. Capers, the tiny buds of the Mediterranean caper bush, are picked by hand, so they tend to be expensive, but they lend a wonderfully piquant flavor.

TOTAL TIME
About 20 minutes

YIELD
4 servings

NUTRITIONAL ANALYSIS PER SERVING

Calories 339.8
Protein 28.9 gm.
Carbohydrates 4.4 gm.
Fat 22.6 gm.
Saturated fat 3.2 gm.
Cholesterol 78.0 mg.
Sodium 399.1 mg.

RAVIGOTE SAUCE

- **2 plum tomatoes (5 ounces), seeded and cut into ¼-inch pieces (¾ cup)**
- **1 tablespoon drained capers**
- **2 to 3 scallions, trimmed and chopped (⅓ cup)**
- **⅓ cup chopped onion, washed in a sieve under cool tap water and drained**
- **2 cloves garlic, peeled, crushed, and chopped (1 teaspoon)**
- **⅓ cup coarsely chopped fresh flat-leaf parsley**
- **½ teaspoon salt**
- **¼ teaspoon freshly ground black pepper**
- **4 tablespoons virgin olive oil**
- **2 tablespoons lemon juice**

- **4 salmon fillet steaks, with all bones, sinews, and skin removed, each 5 ounces and 1¼ to 1½ inches thick**

1 *For the* ravigote *sauce:* Mix all the sauce ingredients together in a small bowl, and set the mixture aside at room temperature.

2 When ready to cook the salmon, bring 3 cups of water to a boil in a stainless steel saucepan. Place the salmon steaks in the pan, and bring the water back to a boil over high heat. (This will take about 2 minutes.) Immediately turn off the heat, or slide the pan off the heat if using an electric stove, and let the salmon steep in the hot liquid for 5 minutes. (The steaks will be slightly underdone in the center at this

point; adjust the cooking time to accommodate thicker or thinner steaks and to satisfy personal taste preferences.)

3 Remove the steaks from the liquid with a large spatula or skimmer, drain them well, and place a steak on each of four warm plates. Sponge up any liquid that collects around the steaks on the plates with paper towels, and spoon the *ravigote* sauce over and around the steaks. Serve immediately.

Green Couscous

Couscous, a staple of North African cuisine, is available now in supermarkets everywhere. Instant couscous is easily reconstituted: just add as much boiling water as there is couscous, and set the mixture off the heat for about 10 minutes.

1 **cup (loose) fresh green herbs (a mixture of chives, parsley, tarragon, and basil)**

2 **cloves garlic, peeled**

1 **cup boiling water**

1 **tablespoon unsalted butter**

1 **cup instant couscous**

½ **teaspoon salt**

1 Place the herbs, garlic, and ¼ cup of the boiling water in the bowl of a blender or mini-chop, and process for about 30 seconds, or until smooth.

2 Heat the butter in a saucepan, and add the couscous and salt. Mix well to coat the couscous with the butter. Add the herb puree and the remainder of the boiling water. Mix well, cover, and set off the heat for 10 minutes.

3 Fluff the couscous with a fork, and serve immediately.

TOTAL TIME
20 minutes

YIELD
4 servings

NUTRITIONAL ANALYSIS PER SERVING
Calories 298.3
Protein 9.5 gm.
Carbohydrates 56.2 gm.
Fat 3.4 gm.
Saturated fat 1.9 gm.
Cholesterol 7.8 mg.
Sodium 284.5 mg.

Chocolate Paris-Brest

Resembling a wheel, this classic French cake is thought to have been created by a Parisian pastry chef to celebrate the famous bicycle race from Paris to Brest, a town in Brittany. The traditional Paris-Brest consists of an almond-topped ring of cream puff dough (choux paste) that is baked, then split and filled with a praline-flavored buttercream. My version of the cake has a chocolate cream filling instead and a garnish of sweetened whipped cream flavored with a little rum.

TOTAL TIME
1½ to 2 hours

YIELD
8 to 10 servings

NUTRITIONAL ANALYSIS PER SERVING

Calories 327.8
Protein 7.1 gm.
Carbohydrates 26.1 gm.
Fat 22.8 gm.
Saturated fat 12.4 gm.
Cholesterol 166.9 mg.
Sodium 84.0 mg.

CREAM PUFF DOUGH

- ¾ cup milk
- 2 tablespoons unsalted butter
- ⅛ teaspoon salt
- ¼ teaspoon granulated sugar
- ¾ cup all-purpose flour
- 3 eggs
- 2 tablespoons sliced almonds

CHOCOLATE CREAM

- ¾ cup milk
- 2 egg yolks
- 2 tablespoons granulated sugar
- 1½ tablespoons all-purpose flour
- 4 ounces bittersweet chocolate, broken into 1-inch pieces

CREAM GARNISH

- 1 cup heavy cream
- 1 tablespoon dark rum
- 1½ tablespoons granulated sugar
- 1 teaspoon confectioners' sugar

1 Preheat the oven to 375 degrees.

2 *For the cream puff dough:* Place the ¾ cup milk, the butter, salt, and the ¼ teaspoon granulated sugar in a saucepan, and bring to a boil over medium to high heat. Remove from the heat, and add the ¾ cup flour in one stroke. Mix well with a wooden spoon, then place back over the heat, and continue to cook, stirring constantly, for 15 to 20 seconds. (The mixture should form a smooth ball.)

3 Place the ball of dough in the bowl of a food processor. Crack the eggs into a small bowl, and mix them well with a fork. Set aside 1 tablespoon of the beaten egg for use as a glaze. Pour about half of the remaining eggs into the processor bowl, and process for about 10 seconds. Add the other half of the eggs, and process for another 15 to 20 seconds, until the eggs are well incorporated and the dough is smooth.

4 Spoon the dough into a pastry bag fitted with a tip with a ¾-inch opening. Pipe a ring with an outside circumference of 8 to 8½ inches on a nonstick cookie sheet. Continue piping adjoining circles of dough inside and on top of the first ring until you have used all the dough and have a a circle that is 1½ to 1¾ inches thick with a hole in the center that measures about 5 inches across. Brush with the reserved tablespoon of egg. Using a fork, mark the surface and sides of the dough, running the tines of the fork gently around the circle to create a lined effect. Sprinkle with the sliced almonds.

5 Place the pastry round in the 375-degree oven, and bake for 20 minutes. Then reduce the heat to 350 degrees, and cook for an additional 35 minutes. (If the pastry begins to brown excessively, cover it loosely with a piece of aluminum foil.) At the end of the cooking period, turn the oven off, and let the pastry remain in the oven for an additional 30 minutes with the door partially open. Let cool to room temperature before removing from the cookie sheet.

6 *For the chocolate cream:* Bring the ¾ cup milk to a boil in a medium saucepan. While the milk is heating, combine the yolks and the 2 tablespoons granulated sugar in a bowl, mixing them with a whisk for about 1 minute. Add the 1½ tablespoons flour all at once, and mix it in with the whisk.

7 Once the milk in the saucepan is boiling, pour it on top of the egg yolk mixture, and mix it in well with a whisk. Return the mixture to the saucepan, and bring to a boil, mixing constantly with the whisk. Boil for 10 to 20 seconds,

(continued)

then remove from the heat, and add the pieces of chocolate. Stir occasionally until the chocolate has melted and is incorporated into the pastry cream. Transfer to a bowl, cover, cool, then refrigerate until ready to use.

8 *For the cream garnish:* Place the cream, rum, and the 1½ tablespoons sugar in a bowl, and whip until stiff.

9 When ready to finish the cake, use a sharp knife to remove a ½-inch-thick horizontal slice, or "lid," from the top, exposing the inside of the cream puff round.

10 Using a spoon, spread the chocolate cream in the bottom section of the pastry round, pushing it gently into the cavities of the pastry. Then, transfer the cream garnish to a clean pastry bag fitted with a ½-inch star tip. Pipe the cream garnish on top of the chocolate cream. Cut the pastry lid into 8 or 10 equal-size pieces, and reassemble these pieces on top of the filled cake. Sprinkle with the confectioners' sugar.

11 At serving time, using the separations on the lid as guides, cut through the bottom half of the cake, and divide into servings.

Tailgate Party

Tomato Potage

Peking-Style Chicken

Corn and Scallion Spoonbread

Chocolate, Walnut,
and Apricot Cookies

Jacques 96

A tailgate party before an early fall football game is a great way to share food and wine with friends. The food should lend itself to the occasion and be easy to handle, serve, and eat. The tomato soup in this menu can be consumed hot from a thermos, and the chicken pieces eaten with the fingers at room temperature along with the spoonbread, which can be dipped into the chicken juices. Enjoy the cookies with a hot cup of espresso.

Tomatoes are always an important part of my late summer and early fall menus. Flavorful and plentiful then, they appear almost daily on my table. Sometimes I serve them plain, right from the garden, sliced and arranged on a plate; sometimes they are the main ingredient in a salad or sauce; and sometimes, as in today's menu, they serve as the inspiration for a soup.

Usually tomato soups of this type are strained before serving to remove seeds and pieces of tomato skin. I find a food mill most effective for this, since it eliminates both the seeds and skin in one step. If you prefer, you can process the soup in a food processor instead; then, either strain it to remove the small pieces of skin and seeds resulting from the processing or eat the soup as is, with this added fiber.

Peking-syle chicken features a mixture of honey, soy, hot pepper sauce, and vinegar, which is brushed on the bird before it goes into the oven to create a flavorful glaze. My family likes the chicken cut

CLAUDINE:
~

"Boston is a great town for tailgating. It doesn't have to be a football game. Fourth of July by the Charles is great: we picnic alongside the river, with food that everybody threw together, and watch the fireworks."

directly through the bones into about twelve small pieces and served on a large platter.

To cut down on your cleaning time afterward, line your roasting pan with aluminum foil. If you don't have a self-cleaning oven, lay some aluminum foil in the bottom of the oven as well.

The spoonbread is good baked in a gratin dish but, for an even fancier presentation, the batter can be baked in individual servings. Spoon the batter into nonstick muffin cups, filling each cup about $2/3$ full, and bake for 18 to 20 minutes. Unmold and serve.

I don't often make cookies, but when I do, I make a double batch and freeze half the finished cookies for later consumption. Wrap them securely, preferably in a double layer of aluminum foil, so they don't pick up the taste of any other foods. They can be eaten almost directly from the freezer, while still half frozen.

WINE & BEER

RED
Beaujolais-Villages

BEER
Apollo Space-Crafted Ale

Apollo Space-Aged Lager

Tomato Potage

A tomato potage is a nice start to a meal, and this recipe couldn't be easier. First, onion pieces are sautéed in olive oil, and a little flour is added as a thickener. Then water is stirred in along with quartered tomatoes, garlic, and seasonings, and the mixture is cooked for 15 minutes. Notice that I use water rather than stock in this soup (and, incidentally, in many of my vegetable soups). Stock tends to overpower some vegetables, and a more natural vegetable taste often is achieved by using water instead.

TOTAL TIME
About 30 minutes

YIELD
6 cups

NUTRITIONAL ANALYSIS PER SERVING
Calories 92.1
Protein 1.4 gm.
Carbohydrates 8.5 gm.
Fat 6.5 gm.
Saturated fat 2.7 gm.
Cholesterol 10.3 mg.
Sodium 286.1 mg.

1 tablespoon virgin olive oil

1 medium onion (4 ounces), peeled and cut into 1-inch pieces (1 cup)

2 teaspoons all-purpose flour

1½ cups water

2 pounds ripe tomatoes, quartered

2 cloves garlic, peeled and crushed

1 teaspoon *herbes de Provence*

1 teaspoon sugar

½ teaspoon freshly ground black pepper

¾ teaspoon salt

2 tablespoons unsalted butter

1 Heat the oil in a large saucepan. When it is hot, add the onion, and sauté it over medium to high heat for 3 to 4 minutes. Add the flour, mix well, cook for 1 minute, then add the water. Mix well.

2 Add all the remaining ingredients except the butter to the saucepan. Bring to a boil over high heat, and stir well. Reduce the heat to low, cover, and cook for 15 minutes.

3 Strain the mixture, pushing it through a food mill fitted with a small screen. Alternatively, emulsify in a food processor, then strain through a conventional strainer, pressing on the solids to retrieve as much of the tomato flesh as possible. (Note: You can omit the straining if you don't object to small pieces of tomato skin and seeds in your soup.)

4 Add the butter, and mix well with a whisk to incorporate it. Serve immediately, or cool, cover, refrigerate, and reheat when ready to serve.

Peking-Style Chicken

This roast chicken is prepared in the style of the famous Chinese Peking duck. Instead of placing the chicken directly in the oven, the conventional approach in most roast chicken recipes, it is blanched first in boiling water. This serve two purposes: it eliminates some of the fat and also tightens the skin on the carcass, making it crisp and beautifully brown when finished in the oven.

TOTAL TIME
About 1½ hours

YIELD
4 servings

NUTRITIONAL ANALYSIS PER SERVING

Calories 564.6
Protein 58.3 gm.
Carbohydrates 9.3 gm.
Fat 31.7 gm.
Saturated fat 8.8 gm.
Cholesterol 177.7 mg.
Sodium 697.6 mg.

- 1 chicken (about 4 pounds), with liver, neck, and gizzard removed
- 1 tablespoon honey
- 2 tablespoons soy sauce
- 1 teaspoon Tabasco hot pepper sauce
- 2 tablespoons balsamic vinegar
- 12 ounces small button mushrooms
- ½ cup water

1 Bring 2½ quarts of water to a boil in a large pot.

2 Meanwhile, remove the wishbone from the chicken. Fold the wings of the chicken behind its back, and truss with kitchen twine to help maintain the bird's tight shape.

3 Lower the chicken, breast down, into the boiling water. Return the water to a boil (this will take about 3 minutes) over high heat. As soon as the water is boiling, reduce the heat to low, and simmer the chicken gently for 5 minutes. Drain, and place the chicken, breast side up, on a rack in a roasting pan or large saucepan.

4 Preheat the oven to 375 degrees.

5 Mix the honey, soy sauce, Tabasco, and vinegar together in a small bowl. Brush the chicken

on all sides with the honey mixture. Roast in the 375-degree oven for 30 minutes.

6 Brush the breast side of the chicken again with the honey mixture, then turn the chicken over on the rack, and brush its back with the mixture. Return the chicken, breast side down, to the oven for an additional 30 minutes.

7 Arrange the mushrooms in one layer under the rack in the pan and add the ½ cup water.

Turn the chicken so it is breast side up again. Brush it with the remaining honey mixture, and return it to the oven for 15 minutes.

8 Transfer the chicken to a platter. Place the accumulated natural juices and the mushrooms in a 4-cup saucepan. Let rest for 2 to 3 minutes, then spoon off as much fat from the surface as possible.

9 Cut the chicken into pieces, and serve with the natural juices and mushrooms.

Corn and Scallion Spoonbread

Prepared with yellow cornmeal and scallions, this spoonbread is easy to make and also reheats well. Best eaten as it emerges puffy and soufflélike from the oven, it is still moist and flavorful after it cools and deflates a little.

TOTAL TIME
50 minutes

YIELD
4 servings

NUTRITIONAL ANALYSIS PER SERVING

Calories 243.3
Protein 13.1 gm.
Carbohydrates 30.6 gm.
Fat 7.4 gm.
Saturated fat 3.2 gm.
Cholesterol 170.5 mg.
Sodium 285.8 mg.

2¾ cups skim or regular milk

¾ cup yellow cornmeal

6 to 8 scallions, cleaned and minced (1 cup)

¼ teaspoon salt

¼ teaspoon freshly ground black pepper

⅛ teaspoon Tabasco hot pepper sauce

3 eggs

2 teaspoons unsalted butter

1 Preheat the oven to 400 degrees.

2 Bring the milk to a boil in a saucepan. Add the cornmeal, and mix well with a whisk. Bring the mixture to a boil, and cook (partially covered to prevent splattering), stirring occasionally, for 3 to 4 minutes. The mixture should be quite thick.

3 Transfer the cornmeal mixture to a bowl, and mix in the scallions, salt, pepper, and Tabasco. Let cool for 10 to 15 minutes.

4 Meanwhile, beat the eggs in a bowl as you would for an omelet, then add them to the cornmeal mixture. Mix in well with a whisk.

5 Butter a 4- to 6-cup round or oval gratin dish, and pour the batter into the dish. Place on a cookie sheet, and bake in the 400-degree oven for 30 minutes, until firm, puffy, and brown. (If you would prefer the spoonbread browner still, place it under a hot broiler for 1 or 2 minutes.)

6 Cut the spoonbread into wedges or squares, and serve immediately.

Chocolate, Walnut, and Apricot Cookies

This oversized version of the traditional chocolate chip cookie also includes nuts and diced, dried apricots. If you prefer, raisins can be substituted for the apricots—either of these dried fruits lends some acidity, which helps counteract the sweetness of the chocolate. Most of this recipe can be assembled in the food processor in just a few minutes, with the chocolate chips, nuts, and dried fruit folded in right before the dough is dropped in large spoonfuls onto a cookie sheet and baked.

⅔ **stick unsalted butter (5⅓ tablespoons)**

3 **tablespoons canola oil**

⅔ **cup light brown sugar**

2 **eggs**

2 **teaspoons vanilla extract**

1⅓ **cups all-purpose flour**

1 **teaspoon baking powder**

⅔ **cup walnut pieces**

⅓ **cup diced (¼-inch) dried apricots**

⅔ **cup semisweet chocolate morsels**

1 Preheat the oven to 375 degrees.

2 Place the butter, oil, sugar, eggs, and vanilla in the bowl of a food processor, and process the mixture for a few seconds, just until smooth. Add the flour and baking powder, and process until they are incorporated and the dough mixture is smooth, about 5 seconds.

3 Transfer the dough to a bowl, and using a wooden spoon or spatula, stir in the nut and apricot pieces and the chocolate chips. For each cookie, drop about 2 tablespoons of dough onto an ungreased cookie sheet, leaving about 2½ inches between the mounds. Bake at 375 degrees for 8 to 10 minutes.

TOTAL TIME
20 to 30 minutes

YIELD
About 20 cookies

NUTRITIONAL ANALYSIS PER SERVING
Calories 156.5
Protein 2.4 gm.
Carbohydrates 19.6 gm.
Fat 8.2 gm.
Saturated fat 2.4 gm.
Cholesterol 25.5 mg.
Sodium 34.7 mg.

Wedding Shower Buffet

Raw Tomato Soup

Open-Face Sandwiches

Frozen Watermelon Slush

Sun Mint Tea

Jacques 96

Claudine has decided to prepare a buffet for the bridal shower of a friend who is going to be married soon. The soup and sandwich spread she is planning will use copious but inexpensive ingredients, and the recipes can all be prepared partially or completely ahead. With forty-eight open face sandwiches, eight cups of soup, and a generous amount of watermelon slush for dessert, there will be enough food to serve eight to ten guests.

The raw tomato soup in this menu can be adapted into a raw tomato sauce for pasta by simply omitting the cup of water. Immediately after the pasta is cooked and drained, add it to the sauce, toss, sprinkle with grated cheese, if desired, and the shredded basil, and serve.

In the twelve sandwich recipes we use four different bread bases. You can limit your bread selections to two, if you prefer, and even substitute other breads more to your liking; but in any case choose fairly dense, compact varieties. This is so you can assemble the sandwiches a few hours ahead without fear that they will absorb moisture from the toppings. Be sure to use lettuce as well; in addition to lending taste and color, it serves as a juiceproof shield between the bread and the other ingredients.

The topping ingredients, which are relatively simple and ordinary, can be purchased several days ahead at almost any supermarket. Much of the preparation can be completed the day before. For example, I would advise you to slice or chop the onion, chives, scallions, and radishes ahead of time. Lined up in front of you in separate receptacles, these ingredients can be sprinkled over the sandwiches.

Many of the products used in the sandwiches, among them herring, anchovies, tuna, smoked mussels, and pimientos, come in cans or jars. Keep your pantry well stocked with these items so that you can make these little sandwiches at a moment's notice. If you prepare all twelve of the sandwich varieties, you might want to use a separate decorative plate for each variety, and arrange the plates around a tureen of the soup set in the middle of the table.

The refreshing watermelon slush, easy to make ahead and to serve, is ideal after the series of sandwiches.

W I N E S

WHITE
Gewurztraminer Hugel

RED
Cambria, Julia's Vineyard,
Pinot Noir

Special Tip

For this type of meal, planning is essential. Make a note of what you have in your refrigerator and pantry. You may discover other possible sandwich toppings that get your creative juices flowing—a dab of liverwurst, slices of apple and Cheddar cheese, maybe even last night's meat loaf or poached fish.

Raw Tomato Soup

This tomato soup is a quick recipe, consisting primarily of garlic and fresh, ripe tomatoes that are first processed together until pureed, then seasoned, and served with a sprinkling of shredded basil.

Although it is acceptable to simply process all the ingredients in a food processor and serve the mixture as such, I find the result smoother and more appealing if the pureed garlic and tomatoes are pushed through a food mill or a conventional strainer to remove tomato skins and seeds before the remaining ingredients are added.

TOTAL TIME
15 minutes

YIELD
About 8 cups

NUTRITIONAL ANALYSIS PER SERVING

Calories 114.9
Protein 1.5 gm.
Carbohydrates 8.1 gm.
Fat 9.4 gm.
Saturated fat 1.6 gm.
Cholesterol 0 mg.
Sodium 290.7 mg.

5 **cloves garlic, peeled**

2½ **pounds very ripe tomatoes, cut into 1-inch pieces (6 cups)**

1 **teaspoon salt**

½ **teaspoon freshly ground black pepper**

½ **teaspoon Tabasco hot pepper sauce**

⅓ **cup peanut oil**

1½ **tablespoons white wine vinegar**

1 **cup water**

½ **cup shredded basil**

1 Place the garlic in the bowl of a food processor, and process it for a few seconds. Add the tomatoes, and process the mixture for 30 to 45 seconds, until pureed.

2 For a smooth soup, push the pureed tomatoes and garlic through a food mill or strain it through a conventional strainer, rubbing as many of the solids as possible through the strainer by pressing on them with the back of a spoon.

3 Add the salt, pepper, Tabasco, oil, vinegar, and water to the pureed mixture, and stir to mix well. Refrigerate until serving time.

4 Spoon into bowls and serve with basil sprinkled on top.

Open-Face Sandwiches

These open-face sandwiches—each consisting of several colorful and complimentary tidbits of food layered on a single thin slice of bread, toast, or a cracker—can be prepared ahead. They are easy and inexpensive to make, especially if you select toppings from what you have on hand.

Salami Sandwiches

4 slices baguette, each about ½ inch thick and 2½ inches in diameter

1 teaspoon unsalted butter, softened

4 slices dry-cured salami (1 ounce total)

4 slices dill pickle (about half a pickle)

Freshly ground black pepper, to taste

1 Spread the baguette slices lightly with the butter. Arrange one salami slice on each bread round, then top with a pickle slice and a sprinkling of pepper.

2 Arrange on a serving plate.

Mozzarella Sandwiches

4 small pieces mozzarella cheese (about 1 ounce total)

4 melba toast rounds (about 2 inches in diameter)

4 pieces red pimiento

1 clove garlic, peeled and thinly sliced

Freshly ground black pepper, to taste

1 Arrange a piece of mozzarella on each melba toast round. Place a piece of pimiento on top, and finish each with a slice of garlic and a sprinkling of pepper.

2 Arrange on a serving plate.

TOTAL TIME
About 2 hours

YIELD
Each recipe makes 4 open-face sandwiches

NUTRITIONAL ANALYSIS PER SALAMI SANDWICH

Calories 59.0
Protein 2.3 gm.
Carbohydrates 4.2 gm.
Fat 3.6 gm.
Saturated fat 1.5 gm.
Cholesterol 8.2 mg.
Sodium 279.3 mg.

NUTRITIONAL ANALYSIS PER MOZZARELLA SANDWICH

Calories 43.3
Protein 2.1 gm.
Carbohydrates 4.8 gm.
Fat 1.7 gm.
Saturated fat 1.0 gm.
Cholesterol 5.5 mg.
Sodium 69.7 mg.

YIELD

Each recipe makes
4 open-face
sandwiches

NUTRITIONAL
ANALYSIS
PER
SCRAMBLED
EGG
SANDWICH

Calories 63.9
Protein 3.7 gm.
Carbohydrates 5.5 gm.
Fat 2.9 gm.
Saturated fat 1.2 gm.
Cholesterol 59.1 mg.
Sodium 186.0 mg.

NUTRITIONAL
ANALYSIS
PER BLUE
CHEESE
SANDWICH

Calories 49.3
Protein 1.8 gm.
Carbohydrates 3.9 gm.
Fat 3.0 gm.
Saturated fat 1.3 gm.
Cholesterol 4.7 mg.
Sodium 117.0 mg.

Scrambled Egg Sandwiches

1   **large egg**

Dash salt

Dash freshly ground black pepper

1   **teaspoon unsalted butter**

1   **tablepoon milk**

4   **slices cocktail pumpernickel bread (2½ inches square)**

1   **slice boiled ham (¾ ounce), cut into julienne strips**

2   **teaspoons chopped fresh chives**

1   Break the egg into a bowl, add the salt and pepper, and beat with a fork.

2   Heat the butter in a small saucepan. Add the egg, and cook it over medium heat, stirring constantly with a whisk, until the mixture is creamy but not dry. Transfer the egg to a bowl, and mix in the milk (which will stop the cooking).

3   Divide the egg over the bread slices. Sprinkle the ham and chives on top. Arrange on a serving plate.

Blue Cheese Sandwiches

4   **slices baguette, each about ½ inch thick and 2½ inches in diameter**

1   **teaspoon virgin olive oil**

¾   **ounce blue cheese (preferably Gorgonzola)**

1   **piece red pimiento, cut into small dice (1 tablespoon)**

1   **tablespoon minced scallions**

1   Preheat the oven to 400 degrees.

2   Brush the baguette slices lightly on both sides with the oil. Arrange them in one layer on a baking sheet, and bake in the 400-degree oven for about 10 minutes, or until nicely browned.

3   Spread the blue cheese on the toasted bread rounds, and top with the pimiento and scallions. Arrange on a serving plate.

Herring Sandwiches

2   Boston lettuce leaves

4   table water crackers (about 2½ inches in diameter)

1   tablespoon sour cream

3   ounces herring in wine sauce (available in 8-ounce jars in specialty food stores and some supermarkets)

2   tablespoons thinly sliced red onion

1   tablespoon chopped fresh chives

1   Break each lettuce leaf in half, and arrange one piece on each cracker.

2   Top each leaf with ¾ teaspoon of the sour cream and 1 or 2 pieces of the herring. Top with the red onion and chives. Arrange on a serving plate.

Tuna Sandwiches

2   teaspoons mayonnaise

1   teaspoon Dijon-style mustard

4   table water crackers (about 2½ inches in diameter)

1   small piece scallion, minced (1 tablespoon)

2   ounces tuna packed in water, drained and broken into 4 pieces

4   oil-cured black olives, pitted

1   Mix the mayonnaise and mustard together in a small bowl. Spread lightly on the crackers, then sprinkle the scallion on top.

2   Arrange one piece of tuna on each cracker, and garnish with an olive. Arrange on a serving plate.

YIELD

Each recipe makes 4 open-face sandwiches

NUTRITIONAL ANALYSIS PER HERRING SANDWICH

Calories 50.8
Protein 2.2 gm.
Carbohydrates 5.1 gm.
Fat 2.2 gm.
Saturated fat 0.8 gm.
Cholesterol 9.4 mg.
Sodium 152.1 mg.

NUTRITIONAL ANALYSIS PER TUNA SANDWICH

Calories 56.9
Protein 4.7 gm.
Carbohydrates 2.6gm.
Fat 2.9 gm.
Saturated fat 0.4 gm.
Cholesterol 7.3 mg.
Sodium 190.7 mg.

YIELD

Each recipe makes
4 open-face
sandwiches

NUTRITIONAL
ANALYSIS
PER HAM
SANDWICH

Calories 54.1
Protein 2.9 gm.
Carbohydrates 4.0 gm.
Fat 2.8 gm.
Saturated fat 0.5 gm.
Cholesterol 5.6 mg.
Sodium 280.0 mg.

NUTRITIONAL
ANALYSIS
PER SMOKED
MUSSEL
SANDWICH

Calories 48.7
Protein 2.6 gm.
Carbohydrates 4.8 gm.
Fat 2.2 gm.
Saturated fat 0.9 gm.
Cholesterol 12.1 mg.
Sodium 94.6 mg.

Ham Sandwiches

4 slices baguette, each about
   ½ inch thick and 2½ inches in
   diameter
1 teaspoon virgin olive oil
1 teaspoon Dijon-style mustard
2 slices boiled ham (1½ ounces
   total), each rolled (from a
   narrow side) and cut in half
4 oil-cured black olives, pitted

1 Preheat the oven to 400 degrees.
2 Brush the baguette slices lightly
   on both sides with the oil.
   Arrange them in one layer on a
   baking sheet, and bake in the
   400-degree oven for about 10
   minutes, or until nicely browned.
3 Spread the mustard on the toasted
   bread rounds, and arrange a piece
   of rolled ham on top. Garnish
   each with a black olive. Arrange
   on a serving plate.

Smoked Mussel Sandwiches

2 leaves radicchio
4 melba toast rounds (about 2
   inches in diameter)
4 teaspoons sour cream
8 smoked mussels (available in
   3½-ounce cans in specialty
   food stores and some
   supermarkets)
1 radish, thinly sliced
Freshly ground black pepper, to
taste

1 Break the radicchio leaves into
   two pieces, and arrange one piece
   on each melba toast round.
2 Spoon 1 teaspoon of sour cream
   on each leaf, and arrange 2
   mussels on top. Place a slice of
   radish on top of the mussels on
   each round, and sprinkle with the
   pepper. Arrange on a serving
   plate.

Anchovy Sandwiches

2 leaves Boston lettuce

4 slices cocktail pumpernickel bread (2½ inches square)

4 teaspoons mayonnaise

1 hard-cooked egg, sliced

4 flat anchovy fillets

1 Break the lettuce leaves into two pieces, and arrange a piece on each bread square.

2 Spoon 1 teaspoon of mayonnaise on top of the lettuce, and add a slice or two of egg. Garnish each with an anchovy fillet.

Smoked Salmon Sandwiches

1½ teaspoons unsalted butter, softened

4 slices cocktail pumpernickel bread (2½ inches square)

8 thin slices unpeeled cucumber (about 1½ ounces total)

4 small slices (about 1½ ounces) smoked salmon

1 tablespoon chopped red onion

2 teaspoons capers, drained

Freshly ground black pepper, to taste

1 Butter the bread slices, then arrange two slices of cucumber on each.

2 Top each with a salmon slice, and sprinkle with the onion, capers, and black pepper. Arrange on a serving plate.

YIELD

Each recipe makes 4 open-face sandwiches

NUTRITIONAL ANALYSIS PER ANCHOVY SANDWICH

Calories 94.5
Protein 4.6 gm.
Carbohydrates 5.4 gm.
Fat 6.0 gm.
Saturated fat 1.1 gm.
Cholesterol 59.7 mg.
Sodium 373.3 mg.

NUTRITIONAL ANALYSIS PER SMOKED SALMON SANDWICH

Calories 54.1
Protein 3.0 gm.
Carbohydrates 5.6 gm.
Fat 2.2 gm.
Saturated fat 1.0 gm.
Cholesterol 6.3 mg.
Sodium 192.0 mg.

YIELD

Each recipe makes
4 open-face
sandwiches

NUTRITIONAL
ANALYSIS
PER SARDINE
SANDWICH

Calories 101.1
Protein 5.6 gm.
Carbohydrates 6.2 gm.
Fat 5.9 gm.
Saturated fat 2.1 gm.
Cholesterol 25.3 mg.
Sodium 145.5 mg.

NUTRITIONAL
ANALYSIS
PER BRIE
SANDWICH

Calories 102.2
Protein 5.6 gm.
Carbohydrates 10.7 gm.
Fat 4.7 gm.
Saturated fat 0.1 gm.
Cholesterol 14.2 mg.
Sodium 205.1 mg.

Sardine Sandwiches

2   leaves spinach

4   slices cocktail rye bread (about 2½ inches square)

4   ounces sardines in tomato sauce (available in 4-ounce cans in specialty food stores and some supermarkets)

Dash salt

2   tablespoons thinly sliced red onion

1½   teaspoons red wine vinegar

1   Break the spinach leaves into two pieces, and arrange one piece of spinach on each of the bread squares.

2   Arrange the sardines with some of their sauce on top of the spinach, salt lightly, and top each with onion slices. Sprinkle with vinegar, and arrange on a serving plate.

Brie Sandwiches

2   Boston lettuce leaves

4   slices cocktail rye bread (about 2½ inches square)

1   small tomato (4 ounces), cut into 4 slices

Dash salt

1   tablespoon thinly sliced onion

2   ounces Brie (or another soft variety cheese), cut into 4 slices

Freshly ground black pepper, to taste

1   Break each of the lettuce leaves into two pieces. Arrange one piece on each bread square.

2   Place a slice of tomato on top of each leaf, then sprinkle each lightly with salt. Top with onion slices, Brie, and pepper. Arrange on a serving plate.

Frozen Watermelon Slush

Although I love watermelon, when I eat the fruit as it is conventionally served, in slices or wedges, I find its seeds troublesome. Here, the seeds are removed ahead, and the flesh of the fruit is pureed and then frozen until solid. A few hours before it is to be served, the mixture is transferred to the refrigerator to soften; then, it's broken into flakes or shavings and spooned into glass goblets or bowls. Delicious and refreshing, it is the perfect dessert on a hot day.

1 medium watermelon (about 12 pounds)

¾ cup lime or lemon juice

¾ cup sugar

1 Cut the watermelon into 2-inch wedges. Remove and discard the rind, black seeds, and as many of the softer white seeds as possible. Cut the flesh into 1-inch chunks, and place them in the bowl of a food processor. Process until liquefied. (Some small chunks may remain.) This will yield about 10 cups. Add the lime juice and sugar, and process just until incorporated.

2 Transfer the watermelon mixture to a stainless steel bowl, cover, and freeze until solid, for 8 to 10 hours.

3 At least 3 to 4 hours (but as long as 5 hours) before serving, move the bowl to the refrigerator to soften the mixture. In the last hour before serving, use a fork to break the softened mixture into shavings. Serve in cold glass goblets or bowls.

TOTAL TIME
About 30 minutes, plus 12 to 14 hours freezer and refrigeration time

YIELD
8 servings

NUTRITIONAL ANALYSIS PER SERVING
Calories 209.6
Protein 2.6 gm.
Carbohydrates 49.9 gm.
Fat 1.8 gm.
Saturated fat 0 gm.
Cholesterol 0 mg.
Sodium 12.1 mg.

un Mint Tea

This is a wonderful use for fresh mint from your garden. Although sun intensifies the flavor of the tea, don't rule out this recipe if two consecutive days of sunshine are not a certainty where you live. You'll get a satisfactory result by setting the jar aside in a warm place indoors for the same amount of time.

TOTAL TIME
2 days

YIELD
12 to 16 glasses

NUTRITIONAL ANALYSIS PER SERVING
Calories 52.3
Protein 0.1 gm.
Carbohydrates 14.2 gm.
Fat 0.1 gm.
Saturated fat 0 gm.
Cholesterol 0 mg.
Sodium 4.9 mg.

3 **tea bags, preferably with good quality black tea**

4 **to 6 cups lightly packed mint leaves**

About 1 gallon cold water

⅔ **cup honey, or to taste**

⅓ **cup lemon juice, or to taste**

Lemon slices, for garnish

1 Place the tea bags and mint in a gallon jar, and fill the jar with the cold water. Cover the jar, and set it in the sun for two days.

2 Strain the tea, season it with the honey and lemon juice, and serve over ice with slices of lemon as a garnish.

Birthday Party for Mom

Ricotta Dumplings with
Red Pepper Sauce

✳

Cornish Hens "Tabaka"

✳

Spinach Salad with Garlic
Dressing

✳

Bread and Butter Pudding

✳

Claudine

For Gloria's birthday party, Claudine wants to cook her mother's favorites. A great portion of this meal can be made ahead, so Claudine can spend time with her mother at the party.

WINES

WHITE

Meursault Perrières 1er Cru

RED

La Crema, Sonoma Reserve, Pinot Noir

CHAMPAGNE

Bollinger, Champagne Special Cuvée Brut

An elegant dish begins the menu: dumplings made with ricotta cheese and served with a red pepper sauce. For the sauce, red pepper and tomato are cut into chunks, cooked in water until tender, strained through a food mill or sieve to remove skin and seeds, then seasoned and thickened lightly with cornstarch. Enhanced with a little unsalted butter and virgin olive oil and emulsified with a hand blender, the vivid red sauce is smooth and rich.

In the main course, a version of a classic Russian main dish, three Cornish hens are cut the length of the backbone, opened but not boned, covered with plastic wrap, and pounded with the base of a heavy saucepan until fairly flat. The hens are then sautéed, mostly skin side down, with a weight on top to compress them further. The idea is to press down on the birds while they cook so their skin, flattened underneath, becomes thin and crispy as it browns. A spinach salad with a garlic-flavored dressing complements the birds.

The dessert, a rich bread and butter pudding, has always been a favorite with my wife, and is what Gloria most often requests to complete her birthday dinner.

Ricotta Dumplings with Red Pepper Sauce

These dumplings are made of ricotta cheese, eggs, Parmesan cheese, and flour—all processed together until smooth—and seasoned with chives. Dropped by spoonfuls into hot water (just under the boil), they cook in about 10 minutes. Not only do the dumplings, creamy white in color, look beautiful with the red sauce spooned over them, but the combined flavors of the sauce and dumplings are wonderfully compatible.

TOTAL TIME
About 45 minutes
(longer if made
ahead and reheated)

YIELD
About 16 dumplings

NUTRITIONAL ANALYSIS PER SERVING
Calories 317.1
Protein 13.4 gm.
Carbohydrates 24.6 gm.
Fat 18.5 gm.
Saturated fat 9.3 gm.
Cholesterol 110.9 mg.
Sodium 713.1 mg.

RED PEPPER SAUCE
- 1 small red pepper (6 ounces), seeded and cut into 1-inch chunks
- 1 tomato (6 ounces), cut into 1-inch chunks
- 1 cup water
- ½ teaspoon salt
- ¼ teaspoon freshly ground black pepper
- 1 tablespoon cornstarch dissolved in 1 tablespoon water
- 1½ tablespoons unsalted butter
- 1 tablespoon virgin olive oil

DUMPLINGS
- 8 ounces ricotta cheese
- ½ teaspoon salt
- ¼ teaspoon freshly ground black pepper
- 1 jumbo egg
- ¼ cup Parmesan cheese, plus additional for sprinkling on the dish at serving time
- ½ cup all-purpose flour
- 2 tablespoons minced fresh chives

1 *For the red pepper sauce:* Place the red pepper and tomato chunks in a saucepan with the 1 cup water. Bring to a boil over high heat, then reduce the heat to low, cover, and boil gently for 8 minutes. Push the mixture through a food mill or sieve to remove the skin and seeds. This will yield 1¾ cups.

2 Return the pureed mixture to the saucepan, and stir in the ½ teaspoon salt, the ¼ teaspoon

pepper, and the dissolved cornstarch. Bring to a boil, then add the butter and oil, and emulsify with a hand blender for about 10 seconds. Keep the sauce warm while you make the dumplings.

3   *For the dumplings:* Bring 3 quarts of water to a simmer (190 degrees) in a pot. Meanwhile, place the ricotta, the ½ teaspoon salt, ¼ teaspoon pepper, egg, Parmesan, and flour in the bowl of a food processor, and process for 10 seconds. Transfer the dumpling batter to a bowl, and mix in the chives.

4   Make the dumplings in two batches, dropping the batter, about 1 tablespoon at a time, as quickly as possible into the hot water. Let the dumplings cook just below the boil at a low simmer (180 to 190 degrees) for 10 minutes. (The dumplings will rise to the top of the water and float as they cook.)

5   After 10 minutes, lift the dumplings from the water with a slotted spoon, drain well, arrange on a platter, and keep warm while you make the remainder of the dumplings.

6   When the second batch of dumplings is cooked, add them to the platter with the first batch, or divide all the dumplings among individual plates. Spoon on the warm red pepper sauce, and serve with a few sprinklings of Parmesan.

Note: To prepare the dumpling first course beforehand, cool the red pepper sauce and refrigerate it. Cook the dumplings as indicated in the recipe through step 4, then transfer them with a slotted spoon from the hot water to a bowl of ice water. When thoroughly cool, drain, arrange in one layer in one large or four individual gratin dishes, cover, and refrigerate until 30 minutes before serving time. Spoon some sauce over the dumplings, sprinkle on about 2 tablespoons of grated Parmesan, and bake in a preheated 400-degree oven for 25 minutes, until the dish is hot and bubbly. Serve with additional warm sauce and grated cheese.

CLAUDINE:

~

"For his birthday, my father's favorite meal is a really good roast chicken, potatoes, and a green salad with a vinaigrette; then, something chocolate for dessert—with Grand Marnier or something elegant. He would love something like that."

Cornish Hens *Tabaka*

Cornish hens *Tabaka* is based on a Russian specialty featuring whole squab chicken that is pressed and sautéed. After the hens are cooked, they are cut in half for serving (half a hen per person). To finish the dish, a natural sauce created from the cooking juices (minus most of the fat) is poured over them, followed by a light sprinkling of fresh lemon juice.

TOTAL TIME
About 45 minutes

YIELD
4 servings

NUTRITIONAL ANALYSIS PER SERVING
Calories 362.5
Protein 37.7 gm.
Carbohydrates 1.3 gm.
Fat 21.9 gm.
Saturated fat 6.2 gm.
Cholesterol 123.6 mg.
Sodium 388.7 mg.

2 **Cornish hens (about 1¼ to 1½ pounds each)**

½ **teaspoon salt**

½ **teaspoon freshly ground black pepper**

2 **teaspoons crushed dried savory leaves**

½ **cup water**

1 **tablespoon lemon juice**

¼ **cup coarsely chopped fresh dill**

1 Cut each hen lengthwise along the backbone, and open it up. Place the hens cut side down on a flat surface covered with plastic wrap, and arrange enough additional plastic wrap on top to cover them.

2 Using a heavy, flat-bottomed pan or a meat pounder, pound the birds until they are flattened to about equal thickness throughout. Sprinkle the skin side of the hens with the salt, pepper, and savory.

3 Heat two large nonstick skillets (each about 12 inches). Arrange the hens, skin side down, in the hot skillets. Cover, and cook for 3 minutes over medium to high heat, then turn the birds over, cover, and cook, skin side up, for an additional 10 minutes. Meanwhile, wrap two bricks (each about 4 pounds) with

aluminum foil; alternatively use cans, heavy saucepans, or even stones.

4   Turn the birds over again in the skillets so they are skin side down, and place a brick on each bird. Cook, uncovered, over medium heat for 20 minutes. The skin on the birds should be well browned and crisp.

5   Remove the birds from the skillets, cut them in half, and arrange the four halves on a platter. Discard all but ½ tablespoon of fat from each skillet, and stir half the water (¼ cup) into each. Bring to a boil, boil for 1 minute, then strain the sauce created in the skillets evenly over the hen pieces on the platter. Sprinkle on the lemon juice and dill, and serve immediately.

Spinach Salad with Garlic Dressing

A plain spinach salad with a garlic dressing is a satisfying accompaniment for the hens. However, the menu can be extended by adding boiled potatoes to the salad, or, if you like, serving a vegetable side dish, too—perhaps steamed carrots or broccoli.

TOTAL TIME
10 minutes

YIELD
4 servings

NUTRITIONAL ANALYSIS PER SERVING

Calories 77.5
Protein 1.4 gm.
Carbohydrates 2.4 gm.
Fat 6.9 gm.
Saturated fat 1.2 gm.
Cholesterol 0 mg.
Sodium 136.2 mg.

1 **package (12 ounces) spinach, preferably young leaves**

GARLIC DRESSING

1 **large clove garlic, peeled, crushed, and finely chopped (about 1 teaspoon)**

2 **teaspoons Dijon-style mustard**

2 **teaspoons red wine vinegar**

⅛ **teaspoon salt**

¼ **teaspoon freshly ground black pepper**

2 **tablespoons peanut, canola, or virgin olive oil**

1 Remove and discard the stems and any damaged or wilted areas from the spinach leaves, and break them into 2-inch pieces. (You should have about 8 loose cups.) Wash the spinach in a basin of cool water, then lift it from the water, drain, and dry thoroughly, preferably in a salad spinner, so no water remains to dilute the dressing.

2 Place all the dressing ingredients in a bowl large enough to hold the greens, and whisk briefly to mix but not emulsify.

3 Add the greens, and toss well. Serve immediately, since the spinach will tend to wilt quickly after it is mixed with the dressing.

Bread and Butter Pudding

This classic British dessert is one of my wife's favorites, especially during the Christmas holidays. Quite easy to make, my version includes candied lemon peel for a delicate citrus taste. The pudding is best served cool (but not ice cold) or at room temperature. Although we prefer it plain, it is often accompanied by whipped cream or vanilla custard cream.

8	strips lemon peel, removed with a vegetable peeler
2½	cups water
⅓	cup granulated sugar
2	cups cold milk
10	thin (⅜-inch) slices from a baguette, preferably 1 or 2 days old
2	tablespoons unsalted butter
⅓	cup golden raisins
2	large eggs
2	egg yolks
1	teaspoon vanilla extract
⅓	cup heavy cream
3	tablespoons sliced almonds
1	teaspoon confectioners' sugar
	Whipped cream, sour cream, or custard cream (optional garnish)

1 Preheat the oven to 375 degrees.

2 Stack the lemon peel strips, one on top of another, and cut them into a thin julienne. (You should have about ¼ cup.) Place the thin strips in a saucepan with 2 cups of the water, and bring to a boil. Boil for 10 seconds, drain in a strainer, and rinse the saucepan and the julienne strips under cool running water.

3 Return the julienned lemon peel to the saucepan with the granulated sugar and the remaining ½ cup water. Bring to a boil, and boil over medium heat for 7 to 8 minutes, until the sugar cooks down to a syrup. Remove the pan from the heat, and add 1 cup of the cold milk. Mix well to dilute the syrup, and set aside.

4 Arrange the bread slices in one layer on a cookie sheet, and place

(continued)

TOTAL TIME
About 1¼ hours

YIELD
4 to 6 servings

NUTRITIONAL ANALYSIS PER SERVING

Calories 348.1
Protein 9.3 gm.
Carbohydrates 34.3 gm.
Fat 19.9 gm.
Saturated fat 10.0 gm.
Cholesterol 217.6 mg.
Sodium 153.4 mg.

in the 375-degree oven for 8 to 10 minutes, until nicely browned. (Do not turn the oven off.) Let cool to lukewarm, and spread the butter generously on the browned side of each slice. Place the slices, buttered side down, in one layer in a 5-cup gratin dish. Sprinkle the raisins on top.

5   Place the eggs and egg yolks in a bowl, and beat with a fork or whisk until well mixed and smooth. Add the vanilla, cream, remaining cup of milk, and the reserved milk–lemon peel mixture. Stir well, and pour over the bread in the dish. Let sit for 15 minutes to allow the bread to soak up some of the liquid.

6   Place the gratin dish on a cookie sheet, and sprinkle the almonds on top. Place in the 375-degree oven for 35 minutes, until set, then place under a hot broiler for 2 minutes to brown the top, if necesary. Cool to room temperature and sprinkle with the confectioners' sugar.

7   Serve the pudding as is, or garnish it with whipped cream, sour cream, or custard cream.

Cuisine d'Amour

Herb and goat cheese soufflé

Veal "blanquette"

Apple and potato purée

Flan "à la Vanille"
with
Caramel-Cognac Sauce

Jacques 96

Often, in part because of language barriers, French cooking seems complicated and difficult to beginning cooks. Yet, if one understands a few basic principles, it can be quite simple.

A soufflé is always a showstopper and generally creates a certain amount of suspense. Some soufflés have to be cooked immediately after assembly, others can wait a while, and some even can be frozen beforehand. The beautifully green and delicate-tasting herb soufflé that begins our menu, for example, can be assembled up to 2 hours before cooking.

Remember, however~regardless of whether the soufflé can or cannot wait before cooking~that once cooked, the soufflé should be served immediately. The old adage is true: The soufflé does not wait for you; you wait for the soufflé.

A veal *blanquette* is the quintessential dish in French bourgeois cooking. Easy to make, it is both impressive and delicious.

Use a soft-fleshed, red-skinned apple (like McIntosh, Rome Beauty, or Macoun) for the apple and potato puree. Trim the apple, and cook it, unpeeled, with the potatoes in a little salted water.

A caramel custard like the one in this menu is still Claudine's, my mother's, and my own favorite dessert. It is versatile in that it can be flavored in such a way as to satisfy the most discriminating palate.

Herb and Goat Cheese Soufflé

The secret to preparing soufflé is timing. When I make this herb soufflé for a family dinner, I prepare the soufflé mixture at my leisure in the afternoon, place it in the mold, and refrigerate it until dinnertime. Then, when I begin to serve apéritifs and set the table, I place the soufflé in a preheated oven. We usually are ready to sit down to eat just when the soufflé is ready for us.

TOTAL TIME
40 to 50 minutes

YIELD
4 servings

NUTRITIONAL ANALYSIS PER SERVING

Calories 340.8
Protein 16.8 gm.
Carbohydrates 14.4 gm.
Fat 24.2 gm.
Saturated fat 11.5 gm.
Cholesterol 307.3 mg.
Sodium 537.7 mg.

2½ tablespoons unsalted butter

3 tablespoons grated Parmesan cheese

1 tablespoon virgin olive oil

¼ cup all-purpose flour

1½ cups milk

½ teaspoon salt

⅛ teaspoon freshly ground black pepper

2 ounces soft goat cheese

2 cups (loosely packed) fresh herbs (a mixture of parsley, basil, chives, and tarragon)

1 large whole egg

4 large eggs, separated

1 Preheat the oven to 375 degrees.

2 Using ½ tablespoon of the butter, butter a 6-cup soufflé dish. Add 2 tablespoons of the grated Parmesan, and shake the dish to coat the bottom and sides with the cheese. Refrigerate until needed.

3 Heat the remaining butter and the oil in a large, sturdy saucepan over medium heat. Add the flour, and mix it in well with a whisk. Add the milk, salt, and pepper, and bring the mixture to a boil over medium to high heat, stirring constantly. Boil for 10 seconds, then add the goat cheese, and mix until smooth. Set aside.

4 Chop the herbs coarsely, then place them in a blender or mini-chop with the whole egg and the 4 yolks from the separated eggs. (Don't use a food

processor—the herbs will be finely chopped, but the mixture will not puree as it will in a blender.) Process until you get a smooth green puree. Add this to the mixture in the saucepan, and mix well. Beat the 4 egg whites in a mixing bowl until they are firm, and fold them into the mixture in the saucepan until well blended.

5 Transfer the mixture in the saucepan to the prepared dish, sprinkle with the remaining tablespoon of Parmesan, and place the dish on a cookie sheet. Bake in the 375-degree oven for 30 minutes, until the soufflé is puffy but still a little runny inside. (Alternatively, refrigerate the soufflé for 2 to 3 hours before baking.) Spoon onto plates, and serve.

CLAUDINE:

"Food is an expression of friendship as well as love. It can set a mood for something more romantic. If the romance isn't there to begin with . . . well, the mood is shot. But if the food is good, at least everybody's going to have a good time."

Veal *Blanquette*

This classic French dish is conventionally thickened with a roux made of butter and flour, and finished with egg yolks and heavy cream. I use lean veal in my recipe; and I break with tradition by thickening it with a mixture of flour and water, called a *blanc,* and eliminating the yolks usually added at the end. Although smooth, rich, and tasty, this veal dish has no fat except for the last-minute addition of cream, which amounts to less than 1½ tablespoons per person.

TOTAL TIME
1 hour 40 minutes

YIELD
4 servings

NUTRITIONAL ANALYSIS PER SERVING
Calories 307.1
Protein 36.2 gm.
Carbohydrates 10.9 gm.
Fat 12.8 gm.
Saturated fat 6.1 gm.
Cholesterol 173.3 mg.
Sodium 927.6 mg.

1½ **pounds veal cubes (each about 1½ inches) from the shoulder, as lean as possible**

¾ **cup water**

½ **cup dry, fruity white wine**

1 **teaspoon salt**

1 *bouquet garni* **(1 rib celery, about 10 parsley stems, 1 large bay leaf, and 2 sprigs fresh thyme, all tied together with string)**

12 **large pearl onions (about 10 ounces), peeled**

16 **button mushrooms (about 8 ounces), washed**

1 **tablespoon all-purpose flour**

2 **tablespoons cool water**

⅓ **cup heavy cream**

6 *cornichons,* **thinly sliced (¼ cup) (see page 111)**

¼ **teaspoon freshly ground black pepper**

2 **teaspoons lemon juice**

1 Place the veal, ¾ cup water, wine, salt, and *bouquet garni* in a sturdy Dutch oven or cast iron casserole. Bring to a boil, uncovered, over high heat, and stir. Add the onions, bring to a boil, reduce the heat to low, and boil gently, covered, for 10 minutes. Add the mushrooms, and cook, covered, for another 5 minutes. Using a slotted spoon, remove the onions and mushrooms, and set them aside in a bowl.

2 Continue to cook the meat, covered, over very low heat (it should boil very gently) for 1 hour 15 minutes, until it is soft, tender, and moist. Remove and discard the *bouquet garni.*

3 Place the flour and 1 tablespoon of the cool water in a small bowl, and mix well with a spoon until smooth and thick. Add the remaining cool water, and mix

well. Pour this flour mixture into the pot with the veal, and mix well. Bring to a boil over high heat, stirring occasionally. Boil gently for 1 or 2 minutes. (At this point, the meat can be set aside in the Dutch oven for a few hours, if desired. Reheat when ready to complete the dish.)

4   Add the cream and the reserved onions and mushrooms to the pot. Bring to a boil over high heat, and stir in the *cornichons,* pepper, and lemon juice. Serve.

Apple and Potato Puree

By the time the potatoes and apple in this recipe are tender and can be mashed together, there is just enough liquid remaining to make the mixture creamy. A whisk or electric hand mixer can be used for mashing, but don't overdo this; the puree should be somewhat chunky, with pieces of apple peel providing a chewy contrast.

1½   **pounds potatoes, peeled and cut into 2-inch pieces**

1   **large McIntosh, Rome Beauty, or Macoun apple (10 to 12 ounces), left unpeeled, but cored and cut into 1-inch pieces**

1   **teaspoon salt**

1¼   **cups water**

2   **tablespoons unsalted butter**

1   Place the potatoes, apple, and salt in a saucepan with the water.

2   Bring the mixture to a boil, cover, reduce the heat to low, and boil gently for 30 minutes, until the potatoes and apple are tender.

3   Add the butter, and mash the mixture by beating it with a whisk or an electric hand mixer until creamy but still somewhat chunky.

4   Serve immediately.

TOTAL TIME
40 minutes

YIELD
4 servings

NUTRITIONAL ANALYSIS PER SERVING
Calories 224.5
Protein 3.2 gm.
Carbohydrates 41.4 gm.
Fat 6.3 gm.
Saturated fat 3.7 gm.
Cholesterol 15.5 mg.
Sodium 421.1 mg.

Flan à la Vanille
with Caramel-Cognac Sauce

This dessert is a sure crowd-pleaser. The sauce is flavored with Cognac here, but rum or Grand Marnier can be substituted, or the alcohol can be omitted entirely. The delicate part of this recipe is the cooking; the flan is cooked in a water bath that should not boil. If it does, the flan will cook too quickly, and when it is unmolded, the exterior of the custard will look like a sponge, with tiny holes all over it.

TOTAL TIME

About 1 hour, plus 5 to 6 hours cooling time

YIELD

6 servings

NUTRITIONAL ANALYSIS PER SERVING

Calories 289.7
Protein 8.6 gm.
Carbohydrates 42.6 gm.
Fat 8.3 gm.
Saturated fat 3.8 gm.
Cholesterol 194.2 mg.
Sodium 103.9 mg.

CARAMEL-COGNAC SAUCE

¾ **cup sugar**

¼ **cup plus ⅓ cup water**

2 **tablespoons Cognac**

1 **tablespoon lemon juice**

CUSTARD

4 **large eggs**

1 **egg yolk**

1½ **teaspoons vanilla extract**

⅓ **cup sugar**

3 **cups milk**

Cookies (optional)

1 Preheat the oven to 350 degrees.

2 *For the caramel sauce:* Mix the ¾ cup sugar and the ¼ cup water together in a heavy saucepan. Bring to a boil over medium to high heat, and boil, uncovered, for 6 to 7 minutes, until the mixture turns a dark blond color. Pour about ¼ cup of the caramel into a 4- to 5-cup soufflé mold, and move the mold so the caramel coats the bottom. (There should be just enough caramel to cover the bottom of the mold.)

3 To the remaining caramel in the pan, add the ⅓ cup water slowly, so as to prevent splattering. When all the water has been added, mix well with a spoon, and bring the mixture back to a boil. Stir again to ensure that all the caramel has melted and there is no thick layer of sugar underneath that might stick to the bottom of the pan. If this occurs, keep stirring until this sugary layer is dissolved.

4 Transfer the caramel to a bowl, and cool it. The mixture will

thicken to the consistency of a heavy syrup. When the caramel is cold, add the Cognac and lemon juice, and stir well. Reserve until serving time. (This sauce can be made ahead and refrigerated in a jar with a tight-fitting lid for several months.)

5 *For the custard:* Place the eggs, egg yolk, vanilla, and sugar in a bowl. Mix well with a whisk, then add the milk, and mix again until it is incorporated. Strain the mixture into the caramel-lined soufflé mold, and place the mold in a saucepan. Add enough water to the saucepan so that it extends about halfway up the outside of the mold.

6 Place the saucepan and mold in the 350-degree oven, and bake for 45 to 55 minutes, until the custard is set in the center. (Check to determine if it is set by inserting the tip of a paring knife into the center of the custard; if the blade comes out clean, the custard is set, even though it may still look and feel soft in the center.)

7 Remove the mold from the water, and let cool for at least 5 to 6 hours (preferably overnight), refrigerated, before unmolding.

8 To unmold the flan, run a sharp knife around the edge, making sure that the knife does not cut into the flan but follows around the inside wall of the mold. Place a platter on top of the flan and invert it, moving the mold gently to dislodge the custard. You will notice that some liquid will come out of the mold as the flan dislodges; discard this thin caramel, and pour some of the thick caramel-Cognac sauce over the custard.

9 Serve the flan with additional caramel-Cognac sauce and, if desired, some cookies.

Pépin Family Favorites

Yankee Inspiration

Clam Fritters

Potato and Watercress
Salad

Broiled Lobster with
Bread Stuffing

Roasted Corn Puree

"Patissière" with Winter Fruit

Jacques 96

Claudine was raised in New England and often likes to eat food that reminds her of her upbringing along its jagged, dramatic coastline.

Clams, lobster, and corn are among her (and my) favorites, especially if we have dug the clams ourselves, as we love to do, purchased our lobster from a local fisherman, and bought our corn from the farm stand down the road.

We start with clam fritters. Large chowder clams, which are ideal here, should be cut into pieces with scissors~this is much easier than slicing through them with a knife.

The potato and watercress salad appears on our table often in the summer. The stem trimmings from the watercress can be used in soups, provided they are of a pureed type that will be strained before serving, since the stems are fibrous.

The rich dessert of pastry cream covered with fruits and glazed with preserves is everyone's favorite. I use mango and kiwi in my version of this classic dessert, but summer berries, ripe pears, or juicy cherries will work just as well in this recipe.

WINE

WHITE

Puligny Montrachet

DESSERT WINE

Stonestreet, Semillon

Clam Fritters

Be sure to reserve all the juice from the clams when opening them; extra juice can be frozen to use in sauces or soups.

Note that the cooked fritters are drained on a wire rack rather than on paper towels (the conventional procedure), because they tend to become soft underneath when placed on paper towels.

TOTAL TIME
About 15 minutes

YIELD
4 servings, about 16 fritters

NUTRITIONAL ANALYSIS PER SERVING

Calories 350.3
Protein 12.7 gm.
Carbohydrates 28.5 gm.
Fat 20.5 gm.
Saturated fat 2.2 gm.
Cholesterol 85.7 mg.
Sodium 396.7 mg.

1 cup shelled clams and 3 tablespoons clam juice, preferably from large quahog or chowder clams (about 1 dozen)

⅔ cup all-purpose flour

⅓ cup yellow cornmeal

1½ teaspoons baking powder

1 jumbo egg

1 large clove garlic, peeled, crushed, and chopped (1½ teaspoons)

4 to 5 scallions, cleaned and minced (½ cup)

1 tablespoon chopped fresh tarragon

¼ teaspoon salt, plus additional for sprinkling (optional)

¼ teaspoon freshly ground black pepper

About 3 cups safflower oil, for deep-frying

1 Using scissors for best results, cut the clams into ½-inch pieces. In a bowl, mix together the flour, cornmeal, baking powder, egg, and enough clam juice to make a smooth batter. Add the clams, remaining clam juice, garlic, scallions, tarragon, salt, and pepper. Mix well.

2 Heat the oil to 375 degrees in a saucepan. Drop about 2 tablespoons of the batter into the hot oil for each fritter, cooking about 8 fritters at a time. Cook the fritters for 4 to 6 minutes, moving them occasionally, until they are browned well on all sides.

3 Lift the fritters from the oil with a slotted spoon, and drain them on a rack. Sprinkle with a little additional salt, if desired, and serve immediately.

Potato and Watercress Salad

Made with the leaves and part of the stems of the watercress, this salad is one of my favorites. I like to use small, unpeeled red potatoes in this recipe, cooking them whole, then cutting them into ½-inch slices. I don't mix the potatoes and watercress until just before serving because watercress tends to wilt quickly.

1   **pound small red potatoes**

2   **bunches watercress**

1   **tablespoon Dijon-style mustard**

¼   **cup peanut oil**

2   **teaspoons soy sauce**

1½   **tablespoons red wine vinegar**

¼   **teaspoon salt**

½   **teaspoon freshly ground black pepper**

1   Remove and discard the eyes and any damaged parts of the potatoes, but do not peel them. Rinse the potatoes well under cold water, place them in a saucepan, and cover with cold water. Bring the water to a boil over high heat, then reduce the heat to medium, and boil gently until the potatoes are tender, 20 to 25 minutes.

2   Drain any water from the potatoes, and spread them out in a large gratin dish to cool. When they are cool enough to handle, cut the unpeeled potatoes into ½-inch slices, and spread the slices out in a single layer (so they are less likely to break) in the gratin dish.

3   Trim the watercress stems, removing about 2 inches from the stem ends and either discarding these ends or setting them aside for use in soup. Wash the trimmed watercress, and dry it thoroughly. (You should have about 3 cups.)

4   Mix the remaining ingredients together in a bowl large enough to hold the finished salad. (Do not worry if these dressing ingredients separate. The mixture should not be emulsified.)

5   At serving time, add the potatoes and watercress to the dressing in the bowl, and toss lightly but thoroughly.

TOTAL TIME
40 minutes

YIELD
4 servings

NUTRITIONAL ANALYSIS PER SERVING
Calories 220.6
Protein 2.9 gm.
Carbohydrates 21.3 gm.
Fat 13.7 gm.
Saturated fat 2.3 gm.
Cholesterol 0 mg.
Sodium 416.2 mg.

Broiled Lobster with Bread Stuffing

I am very fond of broiled as well as grilled lobster and always prepare it both ways at least a few times every summer. I like to blanch lobsters in boiling water for a few minutes before broiling or grilling them; I find that their meat retains its moistness and is more tender as a result. In addition, dropping lobsters into boiling water is one of the fastest ways to kill them.

TOTAL TIME

30 minutes

YIELD

4 servings

NUTRITIONAL ANALYSIS PER SERVING

Calories 348.4
Protein 28.9 gm.
Carbohydrates 20.3 gm.
Fat 14.3 gm.
Saturated fat 4.9 gm.
Cholesterol 105.4 mg.
Sodium 646.7 mg.

4 **lobsters, about 1¼ pounds each (preferably female)**

4 **slices bread from a large country loaf (8 ounces total)**

2 **tablespoons unsalted butter**

2 **tablespoons virgin olive oil**

4 **shallots, peeled and finely minced (1 cup)**

8 **scallions, cleaned and finely minced (1 cup)**

¼ **teaspoon freshly ground black pepper**

Tabasco hot pepper sauce, to taste

½ **cup dry, fruity white wine**

1 Bring 4 quarts of water to a boil in a large pot. When it is boiling, drop in the lobsters, and cover the pan. Cook for about 5 minutes, just until the water returns to a boil. Remove the lobsters from the hot broth, and set them aside until they are cool enough to handle. (The stock can be refrigerated or frozen for use as a soup base.)

2 Toast the bread, then let it cool to room temperature. Break the toast into the bowl of a food processor, and process it into coarse crumbs. This will yield 2 cups.

3 Melt the butter in a medium-size saucepan, and add the oil, shallots, and scallions. Add the bread crumbs, pepper, and Tabasco, and toss lightly. Remove from heat.

4 When the lobsters are cool enough to handle, remove the

claws from each and place them in a plastic bag to prevent splattering as you proceed. Pound the claws with a meat pounder to crack the shells, then either place them as they are on a large jelly roll pan lined with foil, or remove the claw meat intact from the shells, and place it on the foil-lined pans.

5 Preheat the broiler.

6 Split each lobster in half, and remove and discard the stomachs and intestinal tracts from each. Reserve the juices emerging from the lobsters, and combine them with the wine in a bowl.

7 Arrange the lobster body halves side by side and flesh side up next to the cracked claws or claw meat. Lightly fill the body cavities with the stuffing mixture, and sprinkle some of the stuffing on the flesh of the tails. Pour the wine and juice mixture around the lobsters.

8 Place the pan containing the lobsters under the hot broiler on the lowest oven shelf (10 to 11 inches from the heat). Cook for 10 minutes, until the stuffing is nicely browned and the lobsters

are cooked through and hot inside.

9 Arrange two stuffed lobster body halves on each of four plates, and place two lobster claws or the meat from two claws alongside. Spoon some pan juices over the lobsters, and serve immediately.

CLAUDINE:
~

"I love to do a clambake at a beach house. You don't have to wear shoes, and you can get sandy, and you can just have piles of lobsters, crabs, corn, and potatoes— everything on a big table. You can make a mess, and because it's summertime, you can just jump in the water, rinse off, and start again!"

Roasted Corn Puree

This recipe, a combination of cooked cornmeal and caramelized corn kernels, is perfect for corn aficionados. Intense in flavor and chewy, the caramelized kernels can be served on their own.

TOTAL TIME
About 20 minutes

YIELD
4 servings

NUTRITIONAL ANALYSIS PER SERVING

Calories 205.1
Protein 3.4 gm.
Carbohydrates 24.8 gm.
Fat 11.2 gm.
Saturated fat 0.9 gm.
Cholesterol 0 mg.
Sodium 422.1 mg.

3 tablespoons canola oil

2 ears sweet corn, husked and kernels removed (about 1½ cups)

2½ cups water

¾ teaspoon salt

2 large scallions, cleaned and minced (¼ cup)

½ cup yellow cornmeal

1 Heat the oil in a large saucepan, and add the corn kernels. Cook over medium to high heat, covered (to prevent splattering), for about 10 minutes, shaking the pan occasionally and stirring the kernels, until they are nicely browned on all sides. Set aside.

2 Place the water, salt, and scallions in a saucepan, and bring the mixture to a boil over high heat. Add the cornmeal, and cook, partially covered, over medium to low heat for 6 to 8 minutes, stirring occasionally to prevent the mixture from sticking. (The puree should have a smooth consistency.) Add the roasted corn kernels, and mix them in well.

3 Serve immediately.

Patissière with Winter Fruit

This attractive and delicious dessert is essentially a tart without the dough. Although vanilla extract can be used instead of a vanilla bean, I like the taste and look of vanilla bean powder, which appears as little black flecks in the pastry cream. I usually use older (and so somewhat dry) vanilla beans when grinding them to a powder for a recipe. It is a good way of using up older beans, and they tend to create a finer textured powder than soft, fresh vanilla beans.

PASTRY CREAM

- 1 **vanilla bean**
- 3 **tablespoons sugar**
- 1 **cup milk**
- 2 **egg yolks**
- 1½ **tablespoons cornstarch**

GARNISHES

- 1 **ripe mango (about 12 ounces)**
- 1 **kiwi (about 4 ounces)**
- ½ **cup apricot preserves**
- 2 **tablespoons Grand Marnier**
- 1 **tablespoon unsalted pistachio nuts**

Pound cake or cookies (optional)

1 *For the pastry cream:* Break the vanilla bean into pieces, and place it with the sugar in a spice grinder or mini-chop. Process until the mixture is reduced to a powder.

2 Bring the milk to a boil in a saucepan. Meanwhile, combine the vanilla sugar with the egg yolks in a bowl, and stir well with a whisk for about 1 minute. Add the cornstarch, and stir well.

3 Pour the boiling milk on top of the sugar-yolk mixture, incorporate it with the whisk, then place the mixture back in the saucepan. Bring to a boil, stirring constantly with the whisk, and boil for 10 seconds. Place in a bowl, cover with plastic wrap, and cool.

4 Meanwhile, *prepare the garnishes:* Peel the mango, and cut it into

(continued)

TOTAL TIME
About 20 minutes, plus cooling time

YIELD
4 servings

NUTRITIONAL ANALYSIS PER SERVING

Calories 288.8
Protein 4.2 gm.
Carbohydrates 57.0 gm.
Fat 4.9 gm.
Saturated fat 2.1 gm.
Cholesterol 114.9 mg.
Sodium 52.2 mg.

slices. Peel the kiwi, and cut it into slices. In a small bowl, mix the preserves with the Grand Marnier.

5 When the pastry cream is cold, spread it in one layer about 1 inch deep in a nice gratin dish or another attractive serving dish. Arrange the fruit slices on top in one decorative layer. Using a spoon, coat the fruit with the preserves and Grand Marnier mixture, and sprinkle the nuts on top.

6 Spoon the fruit and pastry cream onto individual dessert plates at the table, and serve as is or with a slice of pound cake or cookies.

A tribute to Grandmère

Bread and Onion Soup

Chicken Ragoût Jeannette

"Frisée" with Croûtons

Mémé's Apple Tart

Jacques 96

This menu is truly a walk down memory lane for me. It exemplifies perfectly the simple, unpretentious, flavorful cooking I enjoyed growing up. Some of these tastes I have passed on to Claudine's palate, and some she absorbed while spending summers as a child at her Grandmère Jeannette's house in France.

The soup is best made with fresh or frozen homemade stock, although canned chicken broth, bouillon cubes and water, or even a mixture of water and stock can be substituted. If you use bouillon cubes, however, do so sparingly, since they are very strongly flavored. If you are using canned broth or bouillon cubes and water, or a combination of water and stock, make appropriate adjustments in the amount of salt added based on the saltiness of the liquid.

WINE

RED

Côtes-du-Rhône

The chicken ragoût (or stew) main dish in this menu is typical of my mother's cooking, and this particular mixture and combination of ingredients is the type of food I ate as a child in France. There are lots of onions in the recipe, along with thyme, bay leaves, and other seasonings, and a ltttle flour is added to give some viscosity to the sauce. Green salad is a standard at Mother's house, and *frisée*, a special curly endive, is one of her favorite greens.

My mother's apple pie~famous in the family~is made with a dough of her own invention. Warm milk and baking powder are not conventionally used in tart doughs, but the result is delightful.

Bread and Onion Soup

This soup is an ideal vehicle for leftover bread, which is cut up and browned in the oven first to improve its taste. Grated cheese, one of my mother's favorite additions to the soup, is another great flavor enhancer.

1½ tablespoons peanut oil

2 medium onions (10 ounces), peeled and thinly sliced (about 3 cups)

5 cups unsalted homemade chicken stock

¼ teaspoon salt

½ teaspoon freshly ground black pepper

4 to 5 ounces leftover bread, cut into slices or cubes and baked on a cookie sheet in a 400-degree oven for 10 to 12 minutes

½ cup grated Gruyère cheese

1 tablespoon minced fresh chives

1 Place the oil and onions in a saucepan, and cook over high heat for 8 to 10 minutes, until the onions are nicely browned.

2 Add the stock, salt, and pepper, and bring the mixture to a strong boil.

3 Meanwhile, place the bread cubes in a large soup tureen, and sprinkle the cheese on top. Pour the boiling stock and onion mixture into the tureen, and mix well. Ladle into soup plates, sprinkle the chives on top, and serve immediately.

TOTAL TIME
About 20 minutes

YIELD
4 servings

NUTRITIONAL ANALYSIS PER SERVING
Calories 253.1
Protein 11.5 gm.
Carbohydrates 24.1 gm.
Fat 12.6 gm.
Saturated fat 4.7 gm.
Cholesterol 20.3 mg.
Sodium 964.8 mg.

Frisée with Croutons

This green salad is made with a special curly endive grown and sold now in the United States under the French name of *frisée*. Cultivated specifically so that its leaves are pale (nearly white), mild, and tender, *frisée* usually is costly. Thus, feel free to substitute regular curly endive (selecting specimens with the whitest possible insides) or other greens with flavors you find appealing.

TOTAL TIME
About 20 minutes

YIELD
4 servings

NUTRITIONAL ANALYSIS PER SERVING

Calories 103.9
Protein 1.2 gm.
Carbohydrates 5.5 gm.
Fat 8.6 gm.
Saturated fat 1.2 gm.
Cholesterol 0 mg.
Sodium 203.4 mg.

1½ **ounces leftover bread, preferably from a French baguette loaf, cut into 1-inch pieces (about 1½ cups)**

1 **tablespoon virgin olive, canola, or peanut oil**

DRESSING

1 **tablespoon Dijon-style mustard**

1 **large clove garlic, peeled, crushed, and chopped fine (about 1 teaspoon)**

¼ **teaspoon salt**

¼ **teaspoon freshly ground black pepper**

2 **teaspoons red wine vinegar**

3 **tablespoons virgin olive, canola, or peanut oil**

1 **large or 2 small heads *frisée*, any damaged leaves removed and discarded, and the remainder cut into 2-inch pieces (5 to 6 cups)**

1 Preheat the oven to 400 degrees.

2 Place the bread cubes in a bowl, and sprinkle the tablespoon of oil over them. Toss gently to coat the bread lightly with the oil. Arrange the cubes on a cookie sheet, and bake in the preheated oven for 12 to 14 minutes, until nicely browned on all sides. Set aside.

3 *For the dressing:* In a serving bowl large enough to hold the greens, mix the mustard, garlic, salt, pepper, and vinegar together. Stir in the oil.

4 At serving time, add the salad greens to the bowl containing the dressing. Toss thoroughly, and divide among four salad plates. Sprinkle the croutons on top, and serve immediately.

Chicken Ragoût Jeannette

Salt pork is sometimes called cured pork or sweet "pickle" in this country. In France, this type of meat is called *lard*—hence the name *lardons* for the small pieces of it we add to stews and other dishes. (What we call lard in the United States is called *saindoux* in France.) French *lard* is similar to what the Italians call pancetta, and both of these versions of unsmoked bacon are usually leaner than the salt pork we find in markets here.

Look for a salt pork slab with as much meat on it as possible, then cut it into ½-inch pieces, blanch the *lardons* to remove most of the salt, and sauté them to enhance their flavor. This dish tastes even better when made ahead and reheated at serving time.

TOTAL TIME
About 1 hour

YIELD
4 servings

NUTRITIONAL ANALYSIS PER SERVING
Calories 507.7
Protein 37.0 gm.
Carbohydrates 27.5 gm.
Fat 27.1 gm.
Saturated fat 8.1 gm.
Cholesterol 148.1 mg.
Sodium 731.2 mg.

1 tablespoon canola or safflower oil

4 chicken legs (about 2½ pounds), skin removed (about 2¼ pounds ready-to-cook weight)

1 (4-ounce) piece salt pork, as lean as possible

3¼ cups water

1 bunch scallions (about 6), cleaned and cut into ½-inch dice (⅔ cup)

1 medium onion (6 ounces), peeled and coarsely chopped (1¼ cups)

2 teaspoons all-purpose flour

½ cup dry white wine

2 large cloves garlic, peeled and crushed

½ teaspoon dried thyme leaves

2 bay leaves

½ teaspoon salt

1 pound small red potatoes (8 to 10), left unpeeled, with blemishes and eyes removed

¼ teaspoon Tabasco hot pepper sauce (optional)

2 tablespoons coarsely chopped fresh flat-leaf parsley

1 Heat the oil in a large, sturdy saucepan. When it is hot, add the skinless chicken legs, and sauté them over medium heat for 6 to 8 minutes, turning them occasionally, until they are browned on all sides.

2 Meanwhile, cut the salt pork into ½-inch pieces, and place the pieces in a saucepan with 2 cups of the water. Bring to a boil, and boil for 1 minute. Drain in a sieve, and rinse under cold water.

3 When the chicken is well browned, transfer it to a plate, and add the salt pork pieces (*lardons*) to the drippings in the pan used to cook the chicken. Brown the *lardons,* partially covered (to prevent splattering), over medium heat for 5 minutes, until the pieces are brown and crisp. Add the scallions and onion, mix well, and cook for 5 minutes over medium heat, stirring occasionally. Then add the flour, mix well, and continue browning the mixture over medium heat for 1 minute, stirring occasionally.

4 Add the remaining 1¼ cups water and the wine, and mix well. Then stir in the garlic, thyme, bay leaves, and salt, and bring to a boil, stirring occasionally. Add the potatoes and chicken legs, bring the mixture back to a boil, and boil gently, covered, over low heat for 30 minutes.

5 Remove and discard the bay leaves. Add the Tabasco, if desired, stir, sprinkle with the parsley, and serve.

CLAUDINE:

~

"My grandmother's house in France is a great place. Everybody always sits in the kitchen, even though other places are more comfortable. It's a great house. There's a lot of love there."

Méme's Apple Tart

I remember well the "famous" apple tart my mother made every day as a dessert offering in her small Lyon restaurant, Le Pélican. Unlike any other dough, hers achieved its tender, crumbly, airy texture from the combination of vegetable shortening, baking powder, and warm milk with the flour. I hope you enjoy this taste I associate with food memories from my youth.

TOTAL TIME
1 hour 30 minutes

YIELD
6 to 8 servings

NUTRITIONAL ANALYSIS PER SERVING

Calories 298.8
Protein 2.8 gm.
Carbohydrates 39.8 gm.
Fat 15.1 gm.
Saturated fat 5.0 gm.
Cholesterol 10.1 mg.
Sodium 79.4 mg.

DOUGH

1¼ **cups all-purpose flour**

1 **teaspoon sugar**

½ **teaspoon baking powder**

¼ **teaspoon salt**

6 **tablespoons hydrogenated vegetable shortening (like Crisco)**

¼ **cup milk, heated to lukewarm**

FILLING

2 **pounds Golden Delicious or McIntosh apples (6 medium)**

3 **tablespoons sugar**

2 **tablespoons unsalted butter**

1 Preheat the oven to 400 degrees.

2 *For the dough:* Combine the flour, sugar, baking powder, and salt together in a bowl. Add the shortening, and mix with a spoon or with your hands until the mixture feels and looks sandy. Add the warm milk, and mix rapidly until the dough forms into a ball.

3 Roll the ball of dough between two sheets of plastic wrap to form a circle 11 to 12 inches in diameter, then remove the top sheet and invert the dough into a 9-inch quiche pan with a removable bottom. Use the remaining plastic sheet to gently press the dough into the pan. Remove any dough overhang by rolling your rolling pin across the top edge of the pan.

4　*For the filling:* Peel the apples, quarter them, and remove the cores. Arrange the apple quarters on top of the dough, and sprinkle the sugar evenly over them. Cut the butter into small pieces, and dot the apples with the butter.

5　Place the tart on a cookie sheet, and bake in the 400-degree oven for 1 hour. Cut into wedges, and serve lukewarm.

Mystery Basket

Stuffed Green Peppers

Ziti with Sausage and Vegetables

Butternut Squash Puree

Cream of raspberries and Yogurt

Jacques 76

This menu was prepared on the spur of the moment with ingredients that Claudine brought to my kitchen.

CLAUDINE:

~

"I keep just a few things in my refrigerator: condiments, coffee, and milk. So, when I invite people over, I have to go to the market. It's great to be able to call my father and say, I've bought such-and-such, what do I do with it? He always comes up with something good."

Moist and delicious, stuffed peppers are easy to prepare. All the stuffing ingredients~ground turkey, mushrooms, onions, zucchini, and bread crumbs~are combined with seasonings in a bowl, and this mixture is spooned into the hollowed-out peppers, which are then baked.

Here's a tip about shopping for fresh mushrooms: Instead of selecting mushrooms from the regular produce shelves at the supermarket, walk to the far end of that department or to the back of the store~ wherever there is a rack containing leftover vegetables priced for quick sale. This is where I often find my mushrooms. They may be darker, slightly withered, and open on the underside of the cap (so that you can see the gills), but they will probably have more flavor than the perfect button mushrooms you find in the regular produce area, and they can be bought for a fraction of the price.

As an easy follow-up to the stuffed pepper first course, we have a pasta dish with vegetables. Broccoli, tomatoes, and corn are combined with pasta and a little cooked sausage. The result is colorful and flavorful.

The squash puree, served here as a side dish, makes a great accompaniment for roasted or grilled meat; it can be served as a first course as well.

A simple raspberry and yogurt mixture makes a special finish for this mostly vegetable menu.

W I N E

R E D

Nozzole,
Chianti Classico Riserva

Special Tip

Although I use fresh turkey meat in my stuffed green pepper recipe, I sometimes substitute leftover cooked meat, perhaps from a roast of beef or a stew of lamb or rabbit, that I have on hand. I just chop the meat coarsely and add it, along with any leftover sauce or accompaniments from the original dish, to the stuffing mixture. Hamburger or cold cuts can be used in the same manner as a replacement for the turkey.

Stuffed Green Peppers

As a first course for this menu, I prepare a dish that also could be served as a main course. Green bell peppers, always readily available and relatively inexpensive, are stuffed with ground turkey, vegetables, and fresh bread crumbs made from leftover bread.

TOTAL TIME
1 hour 45 minutes

YIELD
4 servings

NUTRITIONAL ANALYSIS PER SERVING

Calories 496.0
Protein 14.5 gm.
Carbohydrates 35.8 gm.
Fat 33.6 gm.
Saturated fat 11.0 gm.
Cholesterol 48.2 mg.
Sodium 969.0 mg.

4 **large green bell peppers (1¾ pounds)**

10 **ounces lean ground turkey meat**

6 **ounces mushrooms, washed and chopped in food processor (2½ cups)**

5 **ounces leftover bread (2 days old), processed into crumbs in food processor (2½ cups)**

1 **medium onion (6 ounces), peeled and coarsely chopped (1¼ cups)**

1 **small zucchini (4 ounces), cut into ¼-inch dice (1 cup)**

½ **teaspoon salt**

¼ **teaspoon freshly ground black pepper**

1 **tablespoon olive oil**

1 **cup water**

1 Preheat the oven to 350 degrees.

2 Cut around the stem ends of the green peppers, and remove a "hat" from each pepper with the stem in the center. Trim these hats at the base so they are about ½ inch thick, and set them aside. Remove and discard interior seeds, and trim the ribs of the peppers. Stand the peppers upright side by side in a gratin dish.

3 In a bowl, combine the turkey, mushrooms, bread crumbs, onion, zucchini, salt, and pepper, and mix well. Stuff the peppers with this mixture, and replace the reserved hats.

4 Drizzle the olive oil on top of the peppers, and pour the cup of water around them. Place the peppers in the 350-degree oven for 1¼ hours. Serve with the surrounding juice.

Butternut Squash Puree

This simple, smooth, delicious puree is a great garnish or accompaniment for roasted poultry or sautéed veal. It can be served on its own as the vegetable course, or as the first course of a dinner.

1 **butternut squash, about 2 pounds**

1 **clove garlic, peeled**

¾ **teaspoon salt**

¾ **cup water**

½ **cup milk**

1 **tablespoon unsalted butter**

⅛ **teaspoon freshly ground black pepper**

1 Cut the squash crosswise at the base of the neck, dividing it into 2 pieces, then peel both pieces with a sharp knife (this will be difficult) or a vegetable peeler, removing a thick enough layer of skin so there is no green visible on the squash. Halve the body of the squash, remove the seeds with a sharp-edged spoon, and cut the flesh of the squash into 2-inch pieces.

2 Place the squash pieces, garlic, salt, and water in a saucepan, and bring the mixture to a boil over high heat. Cover, reduce the heat to medium, and cook for 20 to 25 minutes, until the squash is tender and there are only 2 to 3 tablespoons of liquid remaining in the pan.

3 Transfer the squash and liquid to the bowl of a food processor, and add the milk, butter, and pepper. Process for 45 seconds to 1 minute, until the mixture is very smooth. Serve immediately, or set aside and reheat in a microwave oven at serving time.

TOTAL TIME
About 40 minutes

YIELD
4 servings (about 3 cups)

NUTRITIONAL ANALYSIS PER SERVING
Calories 131.2
Protein 3.0 gm.
Carbohydrates 24.0 gm.
Fat 4.1 gm.
Saturated fat 2.4 gm.
Cholesterol 12.0 mg.
Sodium 434.9 mg.

Ziti with Sausage and Vegetables

Take advantage of the market when preparing this dish; if good quality cauliflower is less expensive than broccoli, use it instead. Likewise, omit tomatoes entirely if they are too costly, or substitute cherry tomatoes if they are more attractively priced. As for the Italian sausage, look for the best price; sometimes sausage links are less expensive, sometimes patties are cheaper, and sometimes it is more economical to buy sausage packaged in bulk.

TOTAL TIME
30 minutes

YIELD
4 servings

NUTRITIONAL ANALYSIS PER SERVING
Calories 655.8
Protein 23.3 gm.
Carbohydrates 86.9 gm.
Fat 25.3 gm.
Saturated fat 6.8 gm.
Cholesterol 34.3 mg.
Sodium 813.6 mg.

6 **ounces hot and/or mild Italian-style sausage**

2½ **tablespoons virgin olive oil**

12 **ounces pasta (ziti, penne, or rigatoni)**

2 **stalks broccoli (1 pound total)**

1 **tablespoon chopped garlic**

Kernels cut from 2 large ears sweet corn (about 2 cups)

¾ **pound cherry tomatoes, halved if large**

¾ **teaspoon salt**

2 **tablespoons grated Parmesan cheese**

1 Break the sausage into ½-inch pieces, and place it in a saucepan with ½ tablespoon of the oil. Cook over medium heat for about 10 minutes, until most of the fat has emerged from the sausage, and the pieces are nicely browned.

2 Meanwhile, bring 3 quarts of water to a boil in a large saucepan or pot, and add the pasta. Mix well, bring the water back to a boil, and boil the pasta, uncovered, until tender, about 10 minutes (but more or less depending on the type and size of pasta used).

3 While the pasta is cooking, separate the broccoli flowerets from the stalks, and cut the flowerets into 1-inch pieces. Peel the fibrous skin from the exterior of the broccoli stalks, and cut the

stalks into 1-inch pieces. When the sausage has cooked for 10 minutes, add the broccoli to the saucepan, and mix it in well. Then stir in the garlic, reduce the heat to medium, cover, and cook for about 5 minutes.

4 When the pasta is cooked to your liking, scoop out and reserve ½ cup of the cooking liquid, then drain the pasta in a colander. Add the reserved cooking liquid to the sausage and broccoli mixture along with the corn, tomatoes, remaining 2 tablespoons of oil, and the salt. Cover, bring to a boil, and boil for 1 minute.

5 In a large serving bowl, combine the drained pasta with the sausage and vegetables, tossing the mixture together well. Serve with the grated Parmesan.

Cream of Raspberries and Yogurt

This creamy fruit dessert looks much richer than it is. The berries are emulsified with the yogurt to create a smooth, rich-looking, but relatively low-calorie cream.

TOTAL TIME
10 minutes, plus cooling time

YIELD
4 servings

NUTRITIONAL ANALYSIS PER SERVING

Calories 104.7
Protein 2.0 gm.
Carbohydrates 21.6 gm.
Fat 1.7 gm.
Saturated fat 0.9 gm.
Cholesterol 5.5 mg.
Sodium 19.7 mg.

2 **pints ripe raspberries (4 cups)**
¾ **cup plain yogurt**
¼ **cup sugar**
4 **sprigs mint or peppermint**

1 Place about one third of the berries, including any that are less perfect (damaged, wilted, or soft) in the bowl of a food processor with the yogurt and sugar. Process until very smooth. (There still will be small seeds in the mixture; push the puree through a sieve or food mill fitted with a fine screen.)

2 Combine the remaining berries with the raspberry-yogurt sauce, and refrigerate until serving time (as long as 5 to 6 hours). Divide among four dessert dishes, and serve, garnished with mint or peppermint.

Variation: Do not combine the berries and sauce in step 2. At serving time, divide the sauce among four dessert plates, and mound the berries in the center. Top each serving with a sprig of mint or peppermint, and serve.

A CARIBBEAN HERITAGE

Black Bean Soup with Bananas

Cod "à L'Espagnol"

Rice and Cumin

Cucumber and Tomato Stew

Broiled Bananas with Lemon and Sugar

Claudine

Our family table is composed of foods and traditions from France, America, and—for my wife, Gloria, whose ancestry is Puerto Rican and Cuban—the Caribbean.

The black bean soup that begins this menu is inspired by food of the Caribbean. Black beans—more than any other bean variety, I think—make a hearty, savory, and substantial soup. This dish freezes well, and since the work involved is much the same whether I make four or eight servings, I cook a whole pound of beans and freeze half the soup for another day.

I like to garnish this soup with bananas. One of my favorite fruits and a popular recipe ingredient in the tropics, bananas appear again in our dessert. If you aren't as fond of them as I am, substitute a mixture of chopped red onion and hard-cooked eggs as a garnish for the soup.

My wife's Spanish origins make fish a traditional choice for our family at holiday times. The spicy Spanish-style fish featured in this menu is typical of the dishes reflecting her heritage that appear on our Thanksgiving and Christmas tables along with the more familiar turkey with trimmings.

WINES

SHERRY

Antonio Barbadillo,
Medium Dry

WHITE

Kendall Jackson, Vintner's Reserve,
Gewurztraminer

Nothing goes better than rice with piquant dishes like the Cod à *l'Espagnol.* My rice accompaniment is fairly spicy as well, with the assertive flavor of cumin dominating. I use regular long-grain rice that has been converted, or parboiled, so it doesn't get sticky.

The cucumber stew is a reminder of a dish we enjoyed on a recent vacation to the French island of Guadeloupe in the Caribbean. My broiled banana dessert is fast, easy, and works well with almost any menu.

Black Bean Soup with Bananas

I have created several versions of black bean soup through the years, but this one, flavored with pancetta and finished with bananas, ranks at the top of my list of favorites.

TOTAL TIME

About 3 hours, plus 12 hours for soaking the beans

YIELD

8 servings (before freezing)

NUTRITIONAL ANALYSIS PER SERVING

Calories 490.1
Protein 21.2 gm.
Carbohydrates 61.3 gm.
Fat 18.8 gm.
Saturated fat 5.9 gm.
Cholesterol 24.9 mg.
Sodium 1,375.1 mg.

1 pound dried black beans

3 quarts cool water

½ cup (4 ounces) brown rice

8 ounces pancetta or very lean unsmoked or lightly smoked bacon

2 medium onions (12 ounces), peeled and cut into 1-inch pieces

8 cloves garlic, peeled and coarsely chopped (¼ cup)

1 tablespoon *herbes de Provence*

1 tablespoon chili powder

1 (14½-ounce) can diced tomatoes in juice

1 tablespoon salt (less if the pancetta is salty)

2 tablespoons virgin olive oil

2 tablespoons red wine vinegar

1½ teaspoons Tabasco hot pepper sauce

GARNISHES

2 bananas

1 tablespoon lemon juice

¼ teaspoon freshly ground black pepper

1 Remove and discard any debris or damaged beans, and wash the remaining beans well in cool water. Drain the beans, place them in a bowl, cover with cold water, and soak overnight or for 12 hours.

2 Drain the beans, and place them in a pot with the 3 quarts of cool water. Add the rice. Cut the pancetta or bacon into ¼-inch pieces, and add them to the pot. Bring the mixture to a boil over high heat, uncovered (which will take about 20 minutes), stirring occasionally. Skim off and discard any foam that rises to the top. Reduce the heat to very low, cover, and cook for 1 hour.

3 Add the onions, garlic, *herbes de Provence,* chili powder, tomatoes, and salt to the pot, then stir well, and bring to a boil. Reduce the heat to very low, cover, and cook for an additional 1½ hours.

4 Using a hand blender, emulsify the mixture in the pot for about 5 to 10 seconds. (Alternatively, remove 2 cups of the mixture, puree it in a food processor, then return it to the pot.) The object is to thicken the mixture slightly while still maintaining its overall chunkiness.

5 In a small bowl, mix together the oil, vinegar, and Tabasco, then add the mixture to the soup. At this point, remove half the soup, cool to room temperature, cover, and freeze for later consumption.

6 *Prepare the garnishes:* Peel the bananas, and cut them into ¼-inch-thick slices. (You should have about 2 cups). Toss them in a small bowl with the lemon juice and pepper.

7 Divide the hot soup among four bowls. Pass the bananas, and add them to the soup at the table.

Cod à l'Espagnol

I use cod in this recipe, but any fish with firm-textured flesh that separates into large flakes when cooked can be substituted. When cooking cod, take special care, because it tends to dry out if overcooked. Prepared as it is here—with vegetables ranging from green peppers to zucchini and tomatoes—it stays moist and flavorful.

TOTAL TIME
About 20 minutes

YIELD
4 servings

NUTRITIONAL ANALYSIS PER SERVING
Calories 247.4
Protein 31.6 gm.
Carbohydrates 6.3 gm.
Fat 10.4 gm.
Saturated fat 1.5 gm.
Cholesterol 73.1 mg.
Sodium 466.5 mg.

¼ **cup olive oil**

6 **scallions, trimmed (with most of the green left on), cleaned, and minced (¾ cup)**

4 **large cloves garlic, peeled and finely sliced (2 tablespoons)**

1 **green bell pepper, seeded and cut into ½-inch pieces (1¼ cups)**

1 **zucchini (6 ounces), washed and cut into ½-inch pieces (1¼ cups)**

1 **teaspoon salt**

½ **teaspoon freshly ground black pepper**

4 **plum tomatoes (10 ounces), halved, seeded, and cut into ½-inch pieces (1½ cups)**

1 **teaspoon saffron pistils**

4 **pieces cod, each about 1½ inches thick and weighing about 6 ounces**

1 Heat the oil until it is hot but not smoking in a skillet with a lid. Add the scallions and garlic, and sauté them for 1 minute in the oil. Then add the bell pepper and zucchini, and sauté for 1 minute.

2 Add the salt, pepper, tomatoes, and saffron to the skillet, and mix well. Push the pieces of fish into the mixture, completely embedding them in the vegetables. Cover the skillet, reduce the heat to low, and cook the fish for about 10 minutes (more or less depending on the thickness of your fillets). The cod should be just cooked through; overcooking tends to dry it out.

3 Serve immediately.

Rice and Cumin

I like my rice cooked in chicken stock, preferably unsalted homemade stock. If that's what you use, add some salt to this dish.

An ancient spice, cumin is the aromatic dried fruit of a plant in the parsley family. Its assertive, nutty taste lends a distinctive flavor to this rice dish.

TOTAL TIME
30 minutes

YIELD
4 servings

NUTRITIONAL ANALYSIS PER SERVING

Calories 330.7
Protein 7.7 gm.
Carbohydrates 61.9 gm.
Fat 5.3 gm.
Saturated fat 1.1 gm.
Cholesterol 2.8 mg.
Sodium 86.0 mg.

1 tablespoon olive oil

1 medium onion (5 ounces), peeled and chopped (about 1 cup)

1½ cups long-grain converted rice

1 tablespoon ground cumin

3 cups unsalted homemade chicken stock or canned low-salt chicken broth

Salt, to taste

1 Heat the oil in a heavy saucepan with a lid. When the oil is hot but not smoking, add the onion, and sauté for 30 seconds.

2 Add the rice and cumin, and stir well to coat the grains of rice with the oil. Add the chicken stock or broth and salt, if needed, and bring to a boil, uncovered, stirring occasionally, over high heat. Then reduce the heat to low, cover, and cook for 20 minutes. The liquid should be completely absorbed by the rice, which should be tender.

3 Fluff the rice with a fork, and serve immediately.

Cucumber and Tomato Stew

Although popular in many parts of the world, cooked cucumbers are not commonly served in the United States. This recipe, which I first encountered in the French Caribbean, consists of cucumber pieces stewed with tomatoes, onions, and garlic, and finished with cilantro. The taste of this dish is so fresh and delicate that it may persuade Americans to cook this vegetable more often.

2 **tablespoons virgin olive oil**

1 **onion (4 ounces), peeled and chopped (¾ cup)**

4 **scallions, cleaned and minced (½ cup)**

3 **cloves garlic, peeled and sliced (4 teaspoons)**

2 **"seedless" cucumbers, about 1¾ pounds**

5 **plum tomatoes (1 pound), cut into 1-inch pieces (2½ cups)**

1 **teaspoon salt**

½ **teaspoon freshly ground black pepper**

¼ **cup coarsely chopped fresh cilantro**

1 Heat the oil in a large saucepan, and add the onion, scallions, and garlic. Sauté for 1 minute over high heat.

2 Peel the cucumbers, and cut them crosswise into 1-inch rings. (Do not remove the seeds.) Add the cucumber pieces to the saucepan with the tomatoes, salt, and pepper. Cook for about 1 minute over high heat, then stir, cover, and reduce the heat to medium. Cook for 20 minutes.

3 Add the cilantro, mix, and serve.

TOTAL TIME
30 minutes

YIELD
4 servings

NUTRITIONAL ANALYSIS PER SERVING

Calories 128.9
Protein 2.8 gm.
Carbohydrates 15.4 gm.
Fat 7.4 gm.
Saturated fat 1.0 gm.
Cholesterol 0 mg.
Sodium 568.1 mg.

Broiled Bananas with Lemon and Sugar

We finish the meal with bananas broiled with lemon and sugar. The best choice for this dish are bananas with skin that is speckled with black dots, indicating that the fruit is very ripe. Since bananas are often moved to the quick sale rack when they reach this stage of ripeness, look for them there at greatly reduced prices.

TOTAL TIME
10 minutes

YIELD
4 servings

NUTRITIONAL ANALYSIS PER SERVING
Calories 176.7
Protein 1.3 gm.
Carbohydrates 42.5 gm.
Fat 0.5 gm.
Saturated fat 0.2 gm.
Cholesterol 0 mg.
Sodium 6.9 mg.

4   ripe bananas (1½ pounds, about 6 ounces each)
¼   cup fresh lemon juice
¼   cup brown sugar (see Note)
1   tablespoon golden raisins
1   to 2 tablespoons dark rum

1   Preheat the broiler.

2   Peel the bananas, and arrange them in one layer in a gratin dish. Pour the lemon juice over the bananas, and roll them in the juice to prevent them from discoloring. Sprinkle the brown sugar evenly over the bananas.

3   Place the bananas under the hot broiler, about 4 inches from the heat, and broil them until they are brown on top, about 4 minutes. Turn the bananas over, and place them again under the broiler for 3 to 4 minutes, until brown on top. They should be soft at this point when pierced with a fork. Add the raisins.

4   Cool the bananas until they are lukewarm, sprinkle them with the rum, and shake the pan to mix in the rum. Serve immediately.

Note: If your bananas are slightly underripe or you like your desserts very sweet, you may want to add an additional 1 or 2 tablespoons of brown sugar to compensate for tartness.

Claudine's favorite menu consists of food that is hearty, tasty, and assertive in taste, which validates my assumption that childhood food memories are based on taste rather than on presentation.

CLAUDINE:

~

"People ask me a lot what my favorite food is. I don't think I have a favorite food. I think your favorite food depends on what mood you're in. Sometimes your mood is cheeseburgers. Sometimes it's caviar."

The mussels for the first course salad are cooked in a little wine to start. Then, when they are cool enough to handle, they are removed from their shells, combined with a warm potato salad tossed in a vinaigrette dressing seasoned with Dijon mustard, and served on a bed of salad greens.

Here, I offer a bonus: I reserve the cooking liquid from the salad and use it later as the stock for a tasty soup. The extra recipe shows Claudine how, by a little advance planning, the cook can get a leg up on a future meal.

WINES

WHITE

Trimbach Reserve, Pinot Gris

RED

Kendall Jackson, Grand Reserve,
Merlot

A duck is quartered (with carcass bones left attached) and cooked in a skillet for our main dish. When eating this dish at home as a family, we use our fingers as much as our forks—first consuming the meat, then sucking on the flavorful bones. For a fancier service, remove the carcass bones before serving the duck.

To make our classic chocolate dessert a little less rich, I substitute milk for the heavy cream that conventionally serves as its base, combining it with a dash of flour and a little egg to create a light pastry cream. To this pastry cream I add enough chocolate to make a dark, intensely flavored *crème* that can be served with or without cookies.

Mussel and Tomato Soup

If this soup is to be made for a later meal, freeze the stock from the Mussel and Potato Salad (opposite) until you are ready to proceed. If you aren't planning to make the salad, you still can make this fast soup using chicken stock.

The liquid in mussels is never exactly the same. The mussels I cooked for the salad yielded 3 cups of stock, to which I added 1 cup of water. If you get more or less mussel liquid, adjust the water so that there is a total of 4 cups of liquid for the soup.

TOTAL TIME
About 10 minutes

YIELD
4 servings

NUTRITIONAL ANALYSIS PER SERVING
Calories 64.3
Protein 1.9 gm.
Carbohydrates 10.0 gm.
Fat 0.3 gm.
Saturated fat 0.1 gm.
Cholesterol 0 mg.
Sodium 164.8 mg.

1 **(14-ounce) can peeled tomatoes**

4 **cups stock reserved from Mussel and Potato Salad (recipe follows)**

¼ **cup small pasta (tubettini or alphabet)**

4 **scallions, cleaned and cut into ¼-inch pieces (⅓ cup)**

Salt, to taste (amount depending on saltiness of stock)

1 Reserving the juices, break the tomatoes into small pieces.

2 Combine the stock, tomato pieces, and reserved juices in a saucepan. Bring the mixture to a boil, and add the pasta. Cook for a few minutes, just until the pasta is tender, and add the scallions and salt.

3 Boil 1 minute, and serve.

Mussel and Potato Salad

Be sure to wash the mussels several times in cold water, rubbing them against one another with each washing, to rid them of as much sand and dirt as possible. It is not necessary to remove all the incrustations from the shells, since the mussels will be removed from their shells for serving and the shells discarded. Depending on where and the time of year the mussels were collected, they could be very sandy or totally clean when purchased.

3½ **pounds mussels**

½ **cup dry white wine**

½ **cup water**

1 **pound boiling potatoes**

3 **to 4 scallions, peeled and minced (⅓ cup)**

2 **cloves garlic, peeled, crushed, and finely chopped (1 teaspoon)**

DRESSING

½ **teaspoon salt**

1 **teaspoon freshly ground black pepper**

1 **tablespoon Dijon-style mustard**

1 **tablespoon red wine vinegar**

¼ **cup virgin olive oil**

1½ **cups mixed salad greens, rinsed and thoroughly dried**

1 Place the mussels in a large bowl, cover them with cold water, and rub them against one another to scrape off any sandy residue clinging to their shells. Lift the mussels from the water, and transfer them to another bowl of cold water. Repeat the transferring and washing procedure two or three times, discarding the sandy residue in the bottom of each bowl and rinsing it out before refilling it with water each time, until there is no evidence of sand, indicating that the mussels are clean.

2 Place the mussels in a large pot, and add the wine and water. Cover, and bring to a boil over high heat. Toss the mussels in the pan occasionally, and cook them for 2 to 3 minutes longer, covered, to allow them to open.

(continued)

TOTAL TIME
1 hour

YIELD
4 servings

NUTRITIONAL ANALYSIS PER SERVING
Calories 325.5
Protein 16.3 gm.
Carbohydrates 27.3 gm.
Fat 16.3 gm.
Saturated fat 2.3 gm.
Cholesterol 32.4 mg.
Sodium 702.4 mg.

CLAUDINE:

~

"Mussels and French fries are the national dish of Belgium, where I once spent nine months. There are mussels everywhere you go, and everybody makes 'the best' mussels. So I had nine months of eating lots of mussels— that was really wonderful."

A few of the mussels still might not open; with a slotted spoon lift out those that are open, and place them in a bowl while you continue to boil the unopened mussels for 1 to 2 minutes longer to give them another chance to open. Discard any mussels that have not opened at this point. (The cooking of the mussels, from start to finish, should not take more than 12 to 15 minutes.)

3 When the mussels are cool enough to handle, remove them from their shells, and discard any "beard" (resembling dry seaweed) attached to them. Place the mussels in a bowl large enough to hold the finished recipe.

4 Meanwhile, wash the potatoes thoroughly, place them in a large saucepan, and add enough cold water to cover them. Bring the water to a boil over high heat, reduce the heat to low, and boil the potatoes gently, uncovered, until tender, 30 to 40 minutes depending on their size. Drain off any remaining water immediately,

and set the potatoes aside until they are cool enough to handle.

5 Let the stock settle in the large pot for a few minutes, then pour it slowly into a bowl, leaving behind and then discarding any sediment in the pan. You should have about 3 cups of stock. Add enough water to bring the yield to 4 cups, and reserve the stock for use in the mussel and tomato soup (page 250).

6 Peel the lukewarm potatoes, and cut them into ½-inch slices. Add the potatoes to the mussels in the bowl along with the scallions and garlic. Mix all the dressing ingredients together in a small bowl, and add the dressing to the potatoes and mussels. Toss gently to mix.

7 Arrange the salad greens on four individual plates, and spoon the salad onto the greens, dividing it evenly among the plates. Serve at room temperature.

killet Duck

In this easy and delicious recipe, the duck is cooked in much the same way as southern-fried chicken—deep-fried in a covered pot so steam develops, making the meat very moist and tender and the skin crisp. Be sure to use a very large skillet or a saucepan with a lid. The rendered duck fat, a bonus in this recipe, is particularly delicious for sautéing potatoes or flavoring soup.

TOTAL TIME

1 hour

YIELD

4 servings

NUTRITIONAL ANALYSIS PER SERVING

Calories 745.9
Protein 42.0 gm.
Carbohydrates 0 gm.
Fat 62.7 gm.
Saturated fat 21.4 gm.
Cholesterol 185.9 mg.
Sodium 404.0 mg.

1 **duck, about 4½ pounds (defrosted if frozen)**

½ **teaspoon salt**

¼ **cup water**

1 Cut the duck in half lengthwise, slicing through the carcass bones. Then cut each half into two pieces: the leg, and the breast with wing attached. Reserve the neck, gizzard, liver, and heart.

2 Heat a large skillet or saucepan (with a lid), either nonstick or heavy aluminum, until hot. Place the duck pieces skin side down in one layer in the hot skillet. Sprinkle with the salt, dividing it equally among the 4 pieces of duck, and cook over high heat for 5 minutes. At this point, lift the pieces to dislodge them from the bottom of the skillet, and place them, still skin side down, back in the skillet.

3 Add the duck neck and gizzard to the pan, cover, reduce the heat to low, and cook for 15 minutes. (The duck should be cooking in a deep layer of fat and its skin should be very brown at this point.) Reduce the heat to very low, cover, and cook for 30 more minutes. Add the liver and heart, cover, and continue cooking for 5 additional minutes.

4 Remove the duck pieces to a large tray, and keep them warm until serving time in a 170-degree oven. Pour the fat (about 2 cups total) from the skillet into a bowl, remove and reserve 1 tablespoon of it for the green salad (recipe follows), cool, and cover the remainder. (Refrigerated, the fat can be used as needed for up to 2 months for sautéing potatoes or other vegetables.)

5 There should be a small residue of glaze or solidified juices in the bottom of the skillet. Add the water to the skillet, and stir to melt the solidified juices. Reserve 1 tablespoon of the drippings for the green salad (below).

6 Sprinkle the remaining drippings on the pieces of duck and serve with the green salad (below).

Green Salad

Although the duck can be served on its own, with potatoes and a green vegetable, I particularly like it served with slightly acidic salad greens, which help balance the richness of the duck meat.

DRESSING

- 1 tablespoon red wine vinegar
- ¼ teaspoon salt
- ½ teaspoon freshly ground black pepper
- 2 tablespoons peanut or canola oil
- 1 tablespoon rendered duck fat (reserved from Skillet Duck, opposite)

- 5 cups mixed salad greens (romaine, escarole, Boston lettuce, etc.), rinsed and thoroughly dried

- 1 tablespoon duck drippings (reserved from Skillet Duck, opposite)

1 Mix the dressing ingredients together in the bowl in which the salad will be served.

2 At serving time, add the salad greens, and toss well.

3 Divide the salad among four dinner plates, and place a piece of duck alongside the salad on each plate. Sprinkle the reserved drippings on the salad, and serve immediately.

TOTAL TIME
15 minutes

YIELD
4 servings

NUTRITIONAL ANALYSIS PER SERVING
Calories 101.0
Protein 0.9 gm.
Carbohydrates 2.3 gm.
Fat 10.1 gm.
Saturated fat 2.2 gm.
Cholesterol 3.2 mg.
Sodium 143.7 mg.

Crème au Chocolat

This dessert will keep in the refrigerator for a week or so. Be certain to cover it well with plastic wrap, however; otherwise, the chocolate will absorb other flavors in the refrigerator.

TOTAL TIME
About 15 minutes, plus cooling time

YIELD
4 servings

NUTRITIONAL ANALYSIS PER SERVING
Calories 356.5
Protein 9.1 gm.
Carbohydrates 38.4 gm.
Fat 22.6 gm.
Saturated fat 11.6 gm.
Cholesterol 119.1 mg.
Sodium 63.9 mg.

1½ **cups whole milk**
1 **tablespoon instant coffee granules**
1 **whole egg, plus 1 egg yolk**
3 **tablespoons sugar**
1½ **tablespoons all-purpose flour**
6 **ounces bittersweet chocolate, broken into a few pieces**
1 **tablespoon sliced almonds**
Cookies (optional)

1 Preheat the oven to 400 degrees.

2 Bring the milk and instant coffee granules to a boil in a saucepan.

3 Meanwhile, place the egg, egg yolk, and sugar in a bowl, and mix well. Add the flour, and mix it in well.

4 Whisk about 1 cup of the hot milk and coffee into the egg mixture in the bowl, and combine well. Then, pour the contents of the bowl back into the saucepan, and bring the mixture to a boil, stirring constantly with a whisk.

5 Transfer the hot mixture to a bowl, add the chocolate pieces, and mix every 2 or 3 minutes, until the chocolate has melted and is mixed in well. Cool, then refrigerate until serving time.

6 Spread the sliced almonds on a cookie sheet, and place them in the 400-degree oven for 6 to 8 minutes, until they are nicely browned. Set aside.

7 Divide the cold dessert among four dessert bowls or cups. Sprinkle with sliced almonds, and serve with cookies, if desired.

About Jacques Pépin

Jacques Pépin, master chef, food columnist, cooking teacher, and author of fifteen cookbooks, was born in Bourg-en-Bresse, near Lyon. His first exposure to cooking was as a child in his parents' restaurant, Le Pélican. When he was thirteen years old, he began his formal apprenticeship at the distingushed Grand Hotel de l'Europe in his hometown. He subsequently moved to Paris, working at the Meurice, and then at the famed Plaza-Athénée, where he trained under Lucien Diat. Between 1956 and 1958, Mr. Pépin was the personal chef to three French heads of state, Felix Gaillard, Pierre Pfimlin, and Charles de Gaulle.

Moving to the United States in 1959, Mr. Pépin worked first at New York's historic Le Pavillon, then went on to serve as director of research and new development for the Howard Johnson Company, a position he held for ten years. He then helped develop the concept of La Potagerie, a highly successful soup restaurant in New York City. During this period, he studied at Columbia University, earning a master's degree in eighteenth-century French literature in 1972.

Mr. Pépin travels approximately thirty weeks a year, crisscrossing the country to teach his cooking techniques through demonstrations at cooking schools, culinary festivals, and fund-raising events. He appears frequently as a guest personality on radio and TV and was featured on the three-season PBS series, *Today's Gourmet with Jacques Pépin,* which debuted in 1991.

A frequent contributor to newspapers and magazines, he writes a quarterly article for *Food & Wine.* Recent books include *Jacques Pépin's Table* (KQED Books, 1995), which contains all 304 recipes demonstrated on the three seasons of *Today's Gourmet with Jacques Pépin,* and *Jacques Pépin's Simple and Healthy Cooking* (Rodale Press, 1994), a personally illustrated book containing 200 low-fat recipes. His new five-tape set of videos, *Jacques Pépin's Cooking Techniques* (KQED Video, 1996), is a comprehensive guide to the fundamentals of cooking.

Mr. Pépin serves as dean of special programs at the French Culinary Institute in New York City and is an adjunct faculty member at Boston University. He is a founder of the American Institute of Wine and Food, is a member of the International Association of Culinary Professionals, and serves on the board of trustees of the James Beard Foundation. At the 1996 James Beard Awards, he was inducted into the Cookbook Hall of Fame, an honor bestowed each year on one author whose contributions to the literature of food have had a substantial and enduring impact on the American kitchen. He and his wife, Gloria, reside in Madison, Connecticut. Their daughter, Claudine, lives in Boston.

Producer's Acknowledgments

I once worked on a television series where I was warned that when production got under way, it would feel like a fully loaded freight train headed downhill with no brakes. Since then, I've discovered that *most* productions feel like that; the difference is the people who are on board.

The staff and crew of this show were an exceptional group of people, and as we dodged a few slings and arrows of quite outrageous fortune, we discovered a remarkable cohesion of disparate souls, all rising to be their best selves, creating something that is (we hope) worthy of the excellence that Jacques demonstrates with every slice of the knife.

In addition to all the very talented people whom Jacques thanks in his acknowledgments, heartfelt thank-yous go to: camera operators *Harry Betancourt, Greg Overton, Mike Ratusz,* and *Marcial Lopez,* for their sharp eyes and quick reactions. Because of *Birrell Walsh,* we could hear every bit of banter, chop, and sizzle. Technical expertise was coordinated by *djovida* and ably performed by *Eric Shackelford, Bob Sweeney, Dick Schiller,* and *Walt Bjerke.* The smooth flow in the studio was created by *Margaret Clarke, Jim Summers,* and *Peter Borg.* Our beautiful new opening credits (using Jacques' colorful artwork) were designed by *Margaret McCall* and the design group at *Video Arts,* with music by composer and keyboard player *Merl Saunders.* Exterior footage was beautifully shot by *Greg King* with *Helen Silvani* on sound at the *Filoli Center,* the *San Francisco Farmer's Market, Greenleaf Produce, Andronico's Market,* and *Il Fornaio Restaurant.* This was all brought together by editors *Dawn Logsdon, John Andreini,* and *John de Groot.* Our very special thanks go to *Levi Strauss & Co.* for outfitting Jacques and Claudine, and to the *Ritz-Carlton* for housing them in great style.

The great treat for all of us was to see the culinary novice Claudine become a kitchen maven in her own right. A star was born, and it was fun for us all to witness her ascension. I'm sure Jacques' life will never be the same.

—Peggy Lee Scott

WINES PROVIDED BY

Boisset Wines USA

Bordeaux Wine Bureau

Cambria Vineyards & Winery

Cape Ventures

Dreyfus, Ashby & Co.

Frontier Wine Imports

Kendall-Jackson Winery

Kobrand Corporation

Monte Bianco Imports

Rosemount Estate

Seagram Chateau & Estates Wines
    Company

Provins Valais, Sion

Val d'Orbieu Wines

Wine Warehouse

Wines West

FOOD PROVIDED BY

BIRITE Foodservice Distributors

Fresh Fish Company

Greenleaf Produce

Kona Kai Farms

Northern California Unit of the Herb
    Society of America, Inc.

C.J. Olson Cherries

Peet's Coffee & Tea

Preferred Meat

Provimi Veal

Stolt Sea Farm Inc.

Straus Family Creamery

SPECIAL THANKS

All-Clad Cookware

Andronico's Market

Bourgeat USA, Inc.

Braun

Joyce Chen, Inc.

Chicago Cutlery

Corning Consumer Products Company

Draeger's Market

Emile Henry USA Corp.

EuroAmerica Import & Export, Inc.

Filoli Center

General Appliance Berkeley &
    Burlingame

Sandra Griswold

Sue Fisher King

Lamson & Goodnow Mfg. Co.

Levi Strauss & Co.

Meyer Cookware

Now Designs

Oscartielle Equipment, California

Oxo

Ritz-Carlton San Francisco

Doug Rogers

Russell Range

Silver Terrace Nurseries

Tree Spirit

Index

Endive, curly, in *Frisée* with Croutons, 222
Escalopes of Veal in Mushroom and Cognac Sauce, 150–51
Escarole:
    Eggplant, and Olive Sauce, Fusilli with, 88–89
    in Mock Caesar Salad, 32
Etuvée, Broccoli and Rice, 35

F
Figs:
    dried, in Old-fashioned Rice Pudding with Dried Fruit, 44
    in Turkey Roulade *en Cocotte,* 40–41
First courses:
    Apple and Carrot Salad with Yogurt, 138
    Artichoke and Tomato Stew, 158
    Black Bean Soup with Bananas, 240–41
    Bread and Onion Soup, 221
    Clam Fritters, 212
    Cold Corn Soup, 131
    Collard Greens and Yellow Grits Soup, 25
    Cooked Turkey Carcass Soup, 16
    Duck Liver Pâté, 104
    Eggplant Cushions, 48–49
    Frisée with Croutons, 222
    Fusilli with Escarole, Eggplant, and Olive Sauce, 88–89
    Greens and Sardine Salad, 6
    Hard-Cooked Eggs in Mustard Sauce, 42–43
    Herb and Goat Cheese Soufflé, 200–201
    Leek and Gruyère Quiche, 68–69
    Little Corn Dumplings, 130
    Mock Caesar Salad, 32
    Mussel and Potato Salad, 251–52
    Mussel and Tomato Soup, 250
    Polenta and Vegetable *Gâteau,* 148–49
    Potato and Watercress Salad, 213
    Raw Tomato Soup, 178
    Ricotta Dumplings with Red Pepper Sauce, 190–91

Scotch Barley and Mushroom Soup, 58
Steamed Scallops on Spinach with Walnut Sauce, 112–13
String Bean Ragoût, 212
Stuffed Green Peppers, 231, 232
Tomato Potage, 168
Fish, *see names of specific fish and shellfish*
Flan *à la Vanille* with Caramel-Cognac Sauce, 204–5
Flour, measuring and weighing, 66
    see also Pâte
Fondue Soufflé, Warm Chocolate, 94
Fraisage, technique described, 73–74
Frisée with Croutons, 222
Fritters:
    Banana, 28
    Clam, 212
Fromage fort, 31
Frozen Watermelon Slush, 185
Fruit:
    Dried, Old-fashioned Rice Pudding with, 44
    fresh, 15
    soup, 97, 105
    Winter, *Patissière* with, 217–18
    see also names of specific fruits
Fusilli with Escarole, Eggplant, and Olive Sauce, 88–89

G
Galette, Raspberry Cookie Dough, 73–74
Garlic:
    Dressing, Spinach Salad with, 194
    in Mushrooms *en Papillote,* 20
Gâteau, Polenta and Vegetable, 148–49
Gherkins, 111
    see also Cornichons
Ginger and Lemon Chicken, Spicy, 33
Goat Cheese and Herb Soufflé, 200–201
Grapefruit Gratin, 142
Gratin:
    Dauphinois, 64
    Grapefruit, 142
Green beans, *see* String bean(s)
Green Couscous, 159
Green Peppers, Stuffed, 231, 232

Green Salad, 255
Greens and Sardine Salad, 6
Grits, Yellow, and Collard Greens Soup, 25
Gruyère and Leek Quiche, 68–69

H
Ham Sandwiches, 182
Hard-Cooked Eggs in Mustard Sauce, 42–43
Haricots verts:
    about, 118, 128
    in Mixed Vegetable Salad with Toasted Bread Cubes, 132–33
    in String Bean Ragoût, 121
Herb(s, -ed):
    and Goat Cheese Soufflé, 200–201
    in Green Couscous, 159
    Shoulder Steak with, 7
    Yogurt Cheese, 116
Herring Sandwiches, 181
Honey Sauce, Melon and Strawberries in, 52
Hoisin-sesame sauce, in Mock Peking Duck, 100–102

I
Italian sausage:
    in Swiss Chard–Stuffed Onions, 122–23
    Ziti with Vegetables and, 234–35

K
Kalamata olives, 86
    in Fusilli with Escarole. Eggplant, and Olive Sauce, 88–89
    in Potato Slabs with *Tapenade,* 92–93
Kiwi, in *Patissière* with Winter Fruit, 217–18
Kohlrabi, in Corned Beef *Pot-au-Feu,* 114

L
Lamb:
    Breast, Cumin, and Potatoes, 18–19
    leg of, 56–62
        bones from, in Scotch Barley and Mushroom Soup, 58